MAN UP!

SERVANTHOOD
FOR
MEN

Dr. Lee Ann B. Marino, Ph.D., D.Min., D.D.

Man Up!

SERVANTHOOD FOR MEN

Dr. Lee Ann B. Marino, Ph.D., D.Min., D.D.

Published by: *Righteous Pen Publications*
www.righteouspenpublications.com

Unless otherwise noted, Scriptures taken from **The Holy Bible, New International Version®, NIV®,** Copyright © 1973, 1978, 1984, 2011 by Biblica, Inc. ™ Used by permission of Zondervan. All rights reserved worldwide.

Scriptures marked EXB taken from **The Expanded Bible.** Copyright 2011 by Thomas Nelson, Inc. Used by permission. All rights reserved.

Scriptures marked KJV taken from the **Authorized King James Version of the Holy Bible**, Public Domain.

Scriptures marked GW are a copyrighted work of *God's Word to the Nations.* Quotations are used by permission. Copyright 1995 by God's Word to the Nations. All rights reserved.

Scriptures marked ASV are from the **American Standard Version of the Holy Bible,** 1901. Public domain.

Scriptures marked NLT are taken from the **Holy Bible, New Living Translation.** copyright © 1996, 2004, 2007 by the Tyndale House Foundation. Used by permission of Tyndale House Publishers, Inc., Carol Stream, Illinois 60188. All rights reserved.

Scriptures marked AMPC are taken from the **Amplified® Bible, Classic Edition.** Copyright © 1954, 1958, 1962, 1964, 1965, 1987 by The Lockman Foundation. Used by permission." (www.Lockman.org)

Pics in the Public Domain: cover, Cottonbro Studio, Interior: Tima Miroshnichenko, Pexels.com

Book classification:
1. Nonfiction > Religion > Christian Life > Men's Issues.

Copyright © 2017, 2025 by Lee Ann B. Marino

ISBN: 1-940197-39-2
13-Digit: 978-1-940197-39-5

Printed in the United States of America.

"'Well done, my good servant!'
his master replied.
'Because you have been trustworthy
in a very small matter,
take charge of ten cities.'"

(Luke 19:17)

TABLE OF CONTENTS

INTRODUCTION

———————×( )×———————

Sigh. God never lets me do anything "normal."
Earlier this morning, I had no idea I was going to write another book, let alone write this one. Usually, I have an inkling about what I am going to write. Something gives me an idea, a perspective, or think about something else. I usually think about what I am going to write about for at least a few weeks, at most. I have never, ever in all the 20-plus books I have written, started a book hours after the discussion and ideas formed. Yet, here I am, sitting here, staring at the blank page in Microsoft Word, typing away as the inspiration flows and the words come forth, one at a time.

Sometimes, God simply amazes me. This is one of those times.

I finished my last manuscript about six days ago. Even though the Lord has given me some specific writing assignments for this year (that year being 2016), I didn't feel inspired to start any of them. My last manuscript ended three back-to-back works I had completed between October and December. That means in about a period of ten weeks, I wrote well over 350 pages, which should be enough for a normal person to think it's time for a break. For the past week, I did book editing, worked on the January edition of a magazine that will be released at the end of this month, worked on publishing other people's works, and did some cover design. I considered myself to be in between books now, storing up inspiration and energy for the next writing assignment. I wasn't in a hurry. I had 366 days to work on the four books assigned, and in my mind, I was thinking, "No problem!" I figured the inspiration to start a new book (one I already had in mind to write about) would come sometime in the next week or so.

I should have known better, especially since it all started at church this morning. During what turned out to be a very long announcement segment at Sanctuary International

Fellowship Tabernacle - SIFT in Raleigh, North Carolina, we started talking about the "tea party" we want to host for the girls in our church and in our community in April or May of 2016. One of our most involved child members (who was five years old), made the firm declaration that the tea party will be "no boys allowed." I made the joke that I wasn't sure if her grandfather, who was also a church member, was included in the "no boys" rule. He would have to ask his granddaughter about that. It was suggested he could be our butler for the tea party, and we could put a picture online with the caption that says, "At Sanctuary, the men serve the women!" to which I responded, "Oh you know we'll never hear the end of that!" Even though everyone started laughing in good humor and fellowship, we started a mini discussion about the fact that men, as well as women, need to be involved in church and taught how to serve. The underlying message of the discussion was that we are not giving men the idea that they need to be of service, too, and that such is a terrible disservice.

The outcry that I would receive from a scenario like that should not surprise anyone. If we think of the message we give men in church, it is that they should be a certain type of man: loud, strong, stereotypically masculine, in charge, demanding, domineering, and in control of everything, including a woman and family. Men are taught the best way to serve is by being controlling, in charge, or demanding. Remarks are frequently made that men are all leaders, and that women are waiting for the men in their lives and churches to take "the lead," as they call it. If a man is quiet, a good partner, good with his kids, peaceful, artistic, of service to his wife or family, or in any way different from this stereotype, he is spoken of in derogatory terms and accused of not being the role or image of a man that God has "designed" him to be. In the church's efforts to avoid being classified anything different in the world of sexuality or gender, the church is creating an atmosphere where men are increasingly irritated, abusive, and disrespectful to women. Accepting such behavior is, errantly, is considered part of a woman's acceptable service to a man.

Before anyone starts to object, think for a few minutes about the association with "service" in church. We never think of leaders being called to be of service. If anything, we see leaders being served. The people associated with church service are almost universally women: the church mothers, teenage girls who dance or somehow assist the children's ministry, women who teach Sunday School (when was the last time you saw a man in your church in this position?), running the nursery, cleaning the church, the pastor's wife or leaders' wives, female choir members, helps, altar work, and numerous other areas of the church have been designated to women. Even when a woman is in ministry, it is not uncommon to see a woman treated in a very different way than a man and associated with a very different set of standards and expectations. When we think of women, especially in church, we automatically think of "service," and the natural assumption is if they are serving, that the ones women serve are men.

I don't question, nor imply, that there aren't great men of God who serve as they should. Over my nearly 25-year ministry, however, I have never seen as much discord over men, women, gender, and male-female issues as I have the past few years. Even the most innocent-seeming ministers who are the most supportive of women ministers often have the biggest hang-ups about women in their personal lives, being demanding or controlling with their wives or daughters. Many treat their sons more partial than their girls, and I have yet to see a man in ministry who encourages his daughter to follow in his footsteps. The double standard, as we often call it in the secular arena, is alive and well in church. It starts with the basic principle that we do not expect our men to serve in the same way that we expect of our women.

If we, as a church, are serious about doing the work of Jesus, then we should be serious about service. Service is not the job of a gender, but the job of the entire body. This includes men as well as women. In this book, we are going to look in-depth at the different issues keeping men from church service, and how important service is for men if we desire them to become better Christians, husbands, fathers, ministers, and church members.

I recognize that the mere fact I, as a woman, am writing this book is a bit unconventional. There's a part of me that is internally kicking and screaming as I write this (but that'll wear off as I go along.) As I said in the first line of the introduction, God never lets me do anything "normal." I know doing this might not be normal, but it is needed. In my years of ministry, I have always maintained a high male following and have covered men, women, and non-binary individuals in the work of ministry. As a woman, I have spent my life around men as a daughter, sister, girlfriend, wife, employee, friend, minister, business owner, and general human being. I've been around men of all different sorts. I know how they behave. Some men need to sit down while others need to have the right to speak and be who they are without someone trying to change them. I've been there over the years, and I know how awful that feels. I can imagine how awful it must be for men who are pushed to be people they aren't all in the name of faith or a Biblical ideal.

I refuse to disclaim everything I say in this book in the name of "balance" or "objectivity." The second anyone points out inequalities or issues that exist between genders, the arguments start: there isn't male or female in Christ, so we shouldn't talk about it. I agree there is neither male nor female in Christ, but I can't deny that mighty confusing messages are given about gender in church in connection with that statement. I don't question there are women in this world who don't have much use for men or who shirk responsibilities that they have, but I am not advocating that (it is not acceptable for a Christian to "hate" anyone), and I refuse to turn this book into a long discourse of varied perspectives and defenses on what is written here. What I am saying needs to be addressed. In this book it is being addressed for and to men, and for whatever reason, God has given me the revelation that can change the lives of the men who will read and take this advice to heart. That means no apology needs to be given for its contents, and anyone who dislikes the vessel, the message, or the messenger needs to take that before the throne to resolve such issues.

In the church, we have a diverse humanity called out from darkness into the glorious light that only Jesus gives us. As the ultimate servant, men worldwide who call upon the Name of the Savior should aspire to be more like Him. As confused as we often are over just what He did and just Who He was during His walk on this earth, this look at servanthood for men will help us to develop a better understanding and love for Jesus, His sacrifice, and His purpose as men are better able to adopt it in their own lives.

1
NEITHER MALE NOR FEMALE

—————————x( )x—————————

IN CHRIST, THERE IS NO DIFFERENCE BETWEEN JEW AND GREEK [NEITHER JEW NOR GREEK],
SLAVE AND FREE PERSON, MALE AND FEMALE. YOU ARE ALL THE SAME [*OR* UNITED; ONE]
IN CHRIST JESUS.
(GALATIANS 3:28, EXB)

- **Reading assignment:** The Book of Galatians

'm starting this book with a confession. It shocked my current husband, it shocks many who meet me, and it's not something I talk about incessantly, all the time. While at an earlier time in my life I was a bit more aggressive about it than I am today, it's still a truth about me. Ready? Here goes.

I am a feminist.

It probably sounds weird to many that I identify as such. As I said above, I'm not particularly aggressive as a person. I have no problem making dinner for my husband after we've both worked all day. I'm not a particularly political person. Some might say my relationship views borderline (or push beyond) relationship anarchy, but I don't force others to embrace them. Over the years, I've learned the benefit in being temperate in personality rather than extreme. Even my husband doesn't regard me as such, because I'm not "in your face" about it. In contrast with the way feminists are often portrayed in church, such probably doesn't make sense to some. (If that's you, keep reading. Things will make sense in a few minutes.)

Admitting you are a feminist in many Christian circles is worse than admitting you have committed murder. If we listen to the pulpit rants and hostilities of old and young Evangelical men alike who have nothing better to do than complain about changing society, feminists are angry, hostile women who hate men, families, children, and life. Feminists are described as being "hateful," "hate-filled," and full of "hateful" rhetoric. It's seen as the antithesis of what a Christian woman should be: docile, flexible, and willing to do whatever her husband desires. There are many men who would say that you can't be a feminist and a Christian.

History begs to differ. The Bible begs to differ. Millions of Christian women (and some men) for generations beg to differ. I beg to differ.

The word "feminist" is not Latin for "a woman who hates men." Feminism, in its strictest definition, is a term for a person (and that person can be male, female, or of any gender) who believes in the societal and relational equality of men and women. By extension, feminism also extends equality to those of other genders, although it's not always the focus in rights or legislation. It is a radical idea in the sense that women are not considered as subordinate to men and that men do not have an inherited right to dominate women. It is the belief that women are fully capable of making their own decisions, handling money, and making medical choices. Feminists believe a man does not have the right to his will over hers in any circumstance. It gives women responsibility for their lives and decisions and the ability to be accountable for those choices, whatever they may be. Rather than women blaming other people for their actions, feminism gives women the opportunity to be accountable for themselves.

The essence of feminism teaches women they can be anything they desire to be, without hindrance. If a woman wants to be a doctor, lawyer, or minister, that is her choice. She has the ability and capability to do just that. If she wants to be a stay-at-home mom, that is her choice, too. She has the ability and capability to do that. Rather than society or culture dictating a woman's life choices, feminism believes a woman should make her own choice about those things. There is no debate that not all women agree over every secular issue, nor that there is one singular feminist viewpoint on how to be a woman or how to feel about certain secular, social, or political issues. As many feminists as you meet, there are that many opinions about how to handle different women's, life, gender, and family issues.

I don't question there are probably some feminists who hate men, but I know plenty of non-feminists who also hate men. Perhaps more relevant to our topic at hand, I also know plenty of men who, in one form or another, hate women. (We won't even get into the number of men who hate individuals of other genders, for no other reason than they don't understand gender differences.) Some men do hateful, spiteful things to women, and it is understandable why some women adopt that feeling toward men. That doesn't mean hate is automatically a feminist ideology. In fact, studies prove that feminist women often have the best intimate relationships with men. They know enough of themselves and what they want to communicate that to their mates, which helps tremendously in relationship identity. This alone means the idea that feminists hate men is a conjecture, not a reality.

There have been many women who, throughout history, met the definition of "feminist," but didn't identify themselves as such (in most instances, because the term had not yet been invented). The first avowed and acknowledged feminists were the suffragettes of the 1800s and 1900s, women who worked tirelessly to give women the right to vote. Feminism was also largely responsible for abolitionism, women in the professional arena, women's education, and yes, women gaining the right to preach in the pulpit and to be ordained.

These women came to their understanding about the equality of all races and human beings because they studied the Bible. Even though they were rejected by all-male seminaries, those women started their own schools, learned the Hebrew and Greek, and proved themselves worthy for ordination by becoming more competent than their male counterparts in Scriptural matters. By doing so, those women proved that men and women were not just equal in a nice, vague concept, but that they were equal in every sense of the word. This proves women were and are just as competent and eligible for church work and service as any man.

I don't question that starting this first chapter with my discourse on feminism probably raised eyebrows and questions. Feminism nor equality are things we truly understand in church today. It was a strategic move because I want you, as the reader, to examine your response to what I said here. Was it immediate defense? Did you feel disgust? Did you feel like you were being put down or demeaned in some way? The reality is that none of what I said should have instigated such a response. I didn't say men were inferior to women, but that men and women were equal. Yet, too often, whenever we try to discuss the idea of female equality, arguments are always thrown out:

- "These women want a world without men!"
- "These women think they are better than we are!"
- "These radical women think they are superior to us!"

When nothing and no one makes any such assertion, not even close.

When the Bible tells us there is neither male nor female in Christ, it isn't something most men (or women, for that matter) get real excited about. I believe that is because it is not a passage we take literally or as seriously as we should. In the definition I gave above, not only is the Bible an advocate of a feminist viewpoint, but the church should also advocate it, as well. In Christ, in the church, we are supposed to represent a place of service where we are recognized for our love and interaction with each other. None of us are to esteem ourselves too highly. Here, we learn how to lay down our lives not just for our Savior, but each other. That includes men, women, and all genders.

The "ouch" goes right there.

The Bible, feminism and men

If we understand the history of feminism properly, feminism originated in Christianity. While the feminist movement has, over many years, adopted many different ideals (including a secular understanding), the origins of feminism are rooted in the same Bible that Christians espouse, read, and try to emulate. This means that feminism, whether that is a label that someone personally espouses, is an idea that, in concept, anyone who is in church should embody.

That statement is likely shocking to many in the church who conveniently bury the history of both modern Christianity and feminism somewhere concealed, with the hopes that it will never be uncovered. Instead, they use a varied assortment of Biblical passages that seem to accentuate gender inequality, upholding the traditions of men passed off as the Word of God.

However, if someone is truly a Christian, the Bible should not be used as a weapon to promote the elevation of one person and the demoralization of another. The domineering nature of many men and the demoralized nature of many women is so commonplace, we don't even recognize when we hear it in the pulpit. We come into church assuming that men are superior to women according to God's command, and we never give another thought to the things people say in the name of the Bible.

For example: there are several well-known preachers who have said that there is no such thing as marital rape, because the Bible says that a woman's body "does not belong to her, but to her husband." They say that this means a man is entitled to a woman's body, whenever he feels like it, and if he desires sex, he has the right to have sex with her, even if she says she does not want to have it at that time or rejects him.

One well-known preacher who is vehemently against feminism, once read 1 Corinthians 7:1-8 in his congregation. Without reading the entire passage, he got to the section where it says a woman's body is not her own and stopped, saying, "That verse alone denounces every feminist notion out there." The problem is that he didn't narrate the part where it says the husband's body isn't his, either – that passage alone destroys patriarchy. This biased reading of Scripture keeps us from properly understanding the essence of intimate relationships, ensuring abuse and domination are a subtext that's not present in the text itself.

This preacher – and others like him – still believe the ideal that a woman is mere property. They feel she now the property of her husband, to do with her as he pleases. There are also other implied beliefs, such as that men cannot control their sexual drives and urges, that women are disinterested and passive when it comes to sexual matters. To them, enjoyment is for the man, not the woman, and ultimately, women do not have any rights, nor autonomy, over their own bodies.

Rape, or violation of another person using sexual means, is a marital reality for too many women worldwide who often don't have any legal recourse or remedy for such. If a man forces himself on a woman, whether she is his wife or not, that man committed rape. Whether married or not, that man has sinned against his wife and against God, using violence to get his own way, placing his own selfish needs above his wife's well-being.

I don't know if words can express the deeply abusive nature of such a sentiment, or how obvious it is that the people who make these statements have no true concept about God or sacrifice that is required to make marriage work. I don't see how a man, who promises to love and care for his wife throughout their lives, can deliberately violate her body and her wishes. I also don't see how a man can be comfortable with the concept of sexually violating his wife in a most intimate and damaging way, all the while feeling comfortable with it, as if it is some sort of divine right. All of this runs contrary to love, which is supposed to be about concept and sacrifice.

1 Corinthians 7:1-8:

Now I will discuss [concerning] the things you wrote me about [in a letter from the Corinthians; see 8:1; 12:1; 16:1]. It is good for a man not to have sexual relations with [touch; a euphemism for sex] a woman [probably another slogan (6:12; 8:1, 4; 10:23) asserting that a celibate lifestyle was spiritually superior]. But because sexual sin is a danger [of sexual temptations; of sexual sins], each man should have [or have sexual relations with] his own wife, and each woman should have [or have sexual relations with] her own husband. The husband should give his wife all that he owes her as his wife [meet her sexual needs]. And the wife should give her husband all that she owes him as her husband [meet his sexual needs]. The wife does not have full rights [authority] over her own body; her husband shares them. And the husband does not have full rights [authority] over his own body; his wife shares them [revolutionary teaching in the first century, when wives were generally viewed as the possession of their husbands]. Do not refuse to give your bodies to [refuse sex to; deprive] each other, unless you both agree to stay away from sexual relations for a time so you can give your time [devote yourselves] to prayer. Then come together again [resume your sexual relationship] so Satan cannot tempt you because of a lack of self-control. I say this to give you permission to stay away from sexual relations for a time [as a concession/allowance]. It is not a command to do so. I wish that everyone were like me [unmarried], but each person has his own gift from God. One has one gift, another has another gift. (EXB)

The passage commonly cited to justify male privilege for marital rape is found in the passage above, in 1 Corinthians 7:4-5. However, this passage was not talking about marital rape, but celibacy and mutual fasting in a marital situation. In the early centuries of Christianity, asexuality was prized above all other sexual orientations, and many married couples abandoned their marriage relationship to pursue celibacy. They believed such was a higher calling than married life and would result in spiritual purity. The Apostle Paul's advice was that married couples refrain from such thinking. They were inviting temptation into their marriage, asking for trouble. If they were going to enter a period of fasting and prayer, such should be done by the mutual consent of both parties. And, as a reminder, it's also frequently overlooked that the Bible also states a man does not own his own body, but that both should, in marriage, meet the sexual needs of one another.

This Biblical discourse on sex in this specific passage wasn't to validate gender dominance. Rather, it was for both parties in a marriage to recognize their sexual needs and interest. Without outright stating such, Paul – even though it wasn't within his personal understanding – recognized sexual desire in marriage as normal and designed by God. The passage takes away the shame we often associate with sex and create a balance between natural and spiritual things in marriage. It opens the door for marital service, even in a sexual relationship. Both parties were to come together in union, in mutual agreement. It gave both partners certain rights in their intimate relationship. By ideal design, both should desire and want to be with the other, without shame or embarrassment.

The Bible does not give a man (or a woman, for that matter) the right to force himself on his wife for any reason. This passage is not eliminating the different physical, emotional, spiritual, or mental reasons why someone may not be in the mood for sex at any given time. If anything, the Bible establishes through the discourse on prayer and fasting that there will times when a couple is, for whatever reason, abstinent. We can extend this to include situations where there is medical injury or ailment, childbirth, exhaustion, focus on other things, physical discomfort, or any other reason why a couple might not find sex to be the priority in a relationship. If a couple's relationship has a sexual component, it does state such abstinence should only be for a period (not prolonged, as such can create other issues), but it does clarify there will be times in a marriage when a couple does not have sex.

The most ideal situation would be that both partners are, as much of the time as they can be, on the same page about these matters. This passage acknowledges that this does not always happen, however, by emphasizing that both should mutually agree to periods of abstinence. This means that any situation involving sexual abstinence requires communication. We, likewise, recognize communication comes in many forms. If a wife speaks of exhaustion or discomfort, that should be enough to shut down the sexual high for a true servant of the Lord to get her a cup of tea and help her to be comfortable. It should inspire concern, not argument or selfish desire to have one's way.

Using a distortion of the Bible to defend the violation of another person with the Bible's words proves it isn't based on anything Biblical. Instead, it is a Biblical defense used to justify a culture that suits the attitudes and purpose of the individuals who proclaim it. This should disturb us...but often, it doesn't. We start thinking of all the reasons why something like this might happen, and we start justifying it in our minds: maybe she was frigid...maybe she turned him down too much...maybe she did this...maybe she did that...never once do we ever stop and think...maybe what he did was wrong, period.

This might seem like an extreme example, but the reality is that we see this handling of the Bible all the time. Maybe the issues are different, but they are examined with the same abuse and control in mind. Whether it's women's submission, working outside the home, in the pulpit, justifying abuse against women, women are universally subordinate to men, or treating boys differently than we treat girls, we are seeing the Bible used in the same way it is used to justify marital rape: to indicate men have privilege over women, and that men have the right to "cash in" that privilege as they desire.

Feminists are correct when they believe empowering women helps end cycles of abuse and mistreatment. It is just as important in feminism, however, that men are also educated and re-oriented away from ideals such as these.

This means a true understanding of feminist equality is not just about women, but about men as well; about their reorientation and education, and about teaching men about proper treatment and care of women.

Feminism is also about allowing men to be who they are, whether they are society's concept of a "macho man," or not. Because Christianity is the embodiment of different: different ideals, different answers to problems, a different society, and different values, that means that we make room for different in church, including men who are not necessarily society's view of being overly "masculine." I shall address this point more in future chapters.

Patriarchy and the Bible

Several years ago, I had a male assistant. He worked for me as a television producer for my ministry program, *Power for Today*. One day we were talking about the Ephesians 4:11 ministry, which I figured out was extremely threatening to patriarchal mindsets. When I went to discuss this revelation with him, he argued my point. He said there was nothing wrong with patriarchy, because we see patriarchy in the Bible. When I pointed out that patriarchy was never God's intention for humanity, he mumbled to himself, but got quiet, as if he was thinking about what I said (and wasn't at all happy about it). He finally agreed that what I said about patriarchy was true, but he didn't recant his position that patriarchy was a positive thing, or that we should emulate it today.

Patriarchy, as we understand it today, is used in the context of what we could call anti-feminism, or the belief that society, in all its varied forms, should fall under the rule of men. Patriarchy recognizes male authority over the government, working society, and most especially, in the church. In patriarchal rule, each man is the head authority in his household. The wife, children, extended family members, and slaves in that house are under his rule and authority. It's a concept with which most are familiar. As long as that man lives, that household is a representation of him.

16

When he dies, his eldest or next-living male relative becomes the patriarchal leader, to whom those in tow yield, bowing down as the next generational cycle of power begins.

We don't just ascribe patriarchal attitude to the secular world. Patriarchy has become the standard in the American church, who has spread those ideals worldwide. We see each individual church as an autonomous unit, of which the male pastor is the head of that unit. They are seen as having complete and total authority over the beings in that church (which is often seen as a household, of sorts). Whenever it is suggested that perhaps that pastor is not the ultimate authority or that the church experience is larger than that singular local church unit, we are frequently met with intense resistance and hostility.

It is deeply disturbing to me that we have made an entire church model, right down to the way Bible verses are sometimes translated and interpreted and Greek words defined in English, as a complete and total reflection of patriarchal notion and ideal. This shows just how much we look at the Bible in the eyes of our own culture, rather than letting the Bible transform us into what we are supposed to become.

Ephesians 4:11:

And Christ gave gifts to people—He made some to be apostles, some to be prophets, some to go and tell the Good News, and some to have the work of caring for and teaching God's people [He Himself gave apostles, prophets, evangelists, pastors/shepherds, and teachers]. (EXB)

The Bible makes it clear that ministry is more than just for a local church or a man who is over the church. The Ephesians 4:11 ministry is larger than just one man or one church, but has room for all genders within it, all who seek to do the work of servanthood beyond their own immediate understandings. It's not about who is in control, but who is not in control. If we understand God to be behind the work of the church, that means we operate as He calls us, not as we try to orchestrate our own agendas.

God has set up the church in this way because it best helps to ensure church will be about service rather than personal advances for power and control. Whether male, female, or something else, if we are called of Him, then we have the heart and purpose to do His work.

Patriarchy in church goes beyond the mere issue of gender in ministry, however. It relates to the level of control women often feel in their local congregations, the control that a leader will exert, dividing service or available activates by gender, or giving men a certain prominence over women in the church. It also relates to the way in which we understand how the Bible is read, interpreted, and understood.

Before each of us ever read the Bible, we learned the doctrine of the church where we first learned about the Bible. We might have read a few scattered passages here and there, but the consistent message of those we learned from was the doctrine of their belief systems. It was those beliefs they desired to embed within us. We learned, both directly and indirectly, what they wanted us to think the Bible taught and understand the Bible to be a reflection of doctrine, rather than the doctrine to reflect the Bible.

This might sound complex and like nit-picking but accepting what the Bible teaches on patriarchy is very important because we need to see – and understand – patriarchy to be an ideal that is so interwoven into our fabric, that we don't rightly know where it begins, nor ends.

It is true that primitive patriarchy is found in the Bible. This is because the Bible doesn't just stand as a record of doctrine, but of the ideals and concepts believers have had throughout the ages. We traditionally refer to early male Biblical figures as "patriarchs" because they are the founders of our faith. Men such as Abraham and Noah, being the first in their generations to forge ahead with faith, were men who were founders, each in their own right, of spiritual values. This does not mean, however, that patriarchy was ever God's plan for humanity, or that the way we understand patriarchy is proper considering spiritual values. It also doesn't mean that patriarchy was intended to be the plan for the church.

If we look at the entire expanse of Biblical history from Genesis to Revelation, we don't see one viewpoint as pertains to men, women, gender, society, and households. We know what history teaches us about these time frames and the way cultures evolved, but we also see numerous examples of exceptions to those roles in the Bible. Deborah and Lappidoth, Ruth and Naomi, Huldah, and Hosea and Gomer show us obvious examples of their cultural time frames with clear and obvious defiance of culture in their approach to cultural norms. Biblical women led armies, proposed to their husbands, and were instigators in marital separation, as Biblical examples of patriarchal defiance.

The Biblical examples we have that defy ancient patriarchal culture aren't just accidental blips on the radar, thrown in the Bible for good measure for crafty men to avoid. They are found in the Bible to show us a diversity of character, that God did not create women to be subordinate to men, that equality is a real thing as we stand before Him, and that regardless of gender, God will call whoever is best suited to do accomplish His task. In looking at the Bible in this light, we see that His plan for "neither male nor female" has existed since the beginning.

Gender and the Bible

We've heard for several decades about the differences between men and women. There have been studies, books, visions of us on different planets or as different food groups and spoken of as having different "love languages." Most of these ideas have been considered "facts" rather than theories. We don't even consider if all of it is true…much of it is not. Most of it is hype or theory, represented as scientific fact, diluted to such a small level as people try to prove their concepts or ideals with a limited test audience.

I can't deny there are differences between genders. We are different physiologically, created to be different to propagate the species. Anatomically, men and women are not the same. There have also been many studies that prove men and women do not think the same or analyze things in the exact same way. None of this is in question.

We do have to be careful, however, of how far we desire to take this type of thinking and how we process it. Too often we take the perceived differences between men and women to the extreme, making it seem as if we came from two different life sources. What is in question with all these different studies, theories, and ideas is the idea that those differences are as great or life-altering as we might like to think they are. God did not create women to be incapable of thought, nor to create men to be incapable of responsibility. God has not created men and women to be different societally, intellectually, or to have the radically different roles we assign them to have. The differences between men and women were never intended to be a divine punishment for one and an elevation for the other, nor were they ever designed to cause the two sexes to be so isolated from one another. We were designed for companionship, not to approach our relationships with such confusion and with such genuine disdain for one another.

I believe that, on some level, both society and the church often encourage men and women to dislike one another. We've been given the message repeatedly that we're so different, the different traits we have are regarded as antithetical rather than purposeful. We create competition and mean-spiritedness by taunting one another with the abilities each one has, saying the other can't ever have them. We make it seem impossible to communicate, and beyond that, impossible to love. By overly expressing the differences that men and women have, we are missing the whole point of why we have them and why they enhance our lives, the experience of humanity, and make us so much more diverse and rich as people.

Genesis 1:27:

So God created human beings [man; the Hebrew adam can mean human beings, humankind, person, man, or the proper name Adam] in His image [reflecting God's nature/character and representing Him in the world]. In the image of God He created them. He created them male and female. (EXB)

In the garden, God didn't first create a man like we understand the word "man" today; He created humanity. Using the traditional patriarchal language gives us the incorrect idea that God created a literal man rather than a literal human being. Man and woman and everything in between, as humanity, was one. They had joint characteristics, a joint body, joint thoughts and formed a joint unit. From humanity, God then separated humanity into male and female, creating Adam and separating Eve from Adam, and commissioning them to dwell in productivity and continue humanity.

What we tend to overlook is that people of every gender have the same origin. They were taken one from the other and are created with the same status before God: equal in His eyes, created in His image likeness. Women, men, and everyone else was created to know their Creator and represent Him on this earth. We are of the same stock, the same creation, and the same purpose. The differences have now were once shared. Some of those differences aren't as far apart as we might think. The stereotypes we extend to men and women are characteristics that the other sex has, by virtue of creation, whether they are strong in them, or not. People are not stereotypes, and being uniquely created by God means that those gender-specific characteristics we often like to fall back on are nothing more than societal stereotyping.

In salvation, we recognize that Jesus' sacrifice was sufficient to overcome sin and death. In essence, Jesus started the process toward restoring all things and returning us back to the beginning. That means when we start talking about there being neither male nor female, we are living a Biblical prophecy of returning to the garden, prior to sin's entry in the world. While we still carry the idea of biological sex and societal gender in our own bodies, we are something else in Christ. We are one again, neither competing, nor arguing, being willing to lay down our lives for one another and doing the work of the Lord.

In other words: any Bible verse that seems to emphasize gender needs to be taken in the light of salvation, not the flesh. It is easy to read any passage of the Bible in the flesh and try to interpret it as such, but the Bible's purpose is not to make us more self-centered and arrogant. If there is a passage that appeals to us on a level of allowing us to remain in the flesh and appeal to the notion that one person, group, gender, or ideal is superior to another, then we are missing the point of the Scripture and most definitely, God's intent in that passage.

As believers, it is our job to strive beyond male and female and beyond the different worldly ideals that keep us bound, judgmental, and hard. God desires us to embody certain ideals that draw people, rather than deter them. As Christians, it benefits all of us to look into our hearts and see what we say to others, especially if we are close to them.

<u>Reflections</u>

- How do you feel about the women in your life, in a general sense? Do you see them as people?

- How do you feel when a woman you know makes a decision you don't agree with?

- Do you believe the relationship between genders is antagonistic? Why or why not?

2
"ALPHA MALE SYNDROME" AND THE CHURCH

—————————=)( )(=—————————

IN EVERYTHING SET THEM AN EXAMPLE BY DOING WHAT IS GOOD.
IN YOUR TEACHING SHOW INTEGRITY, SERIOUSNESS AND SOUNDNESS OF SPEECH
THAT CANNOT BE CONDEMNED, SO THAT THOSE WHO OPPOSE YOU MAY BE ASHAMED
BECAUSE THEY HAVE NOTHING BAD TO SAY ABOUT US.
(TITUS 2:7-8)

- **Reading assignment:** The Book of Ephesians

For all who are curious as to the point of the last chapter, do not despair: you are about to learn! The point of the last chapter, with my explanations of feminist history, feminism and the Bible, patriarchy and gender and the Bible was simple. I included such there first so those who are reading this book could take some time and discern the thoughts and ideas of their own hearts. The Bible tells us God knows what goes on in our hearts (within our innermost being), and it is pretty obvious if we listen to couples in church that there are a lot of issues between couples that don't seem to get resolved. This is especially true in male-female relationships. Women are often angry because they feel excluded from church and men are angry because they feel women are taking over church. Both sides feel the other doesn't understand or listen.

Unfortunately, the church isn't helping with these issues. If anything, it's often fostering them. It's not uncommon to hear preaching that delegates women to a certain role, then see the rallying cries of men who are encouraged to adopt a certain role. Through men's meetings, conferences, gendered gift packages, and sometimes outright suggestion, we see attitudes that cause a further rift between men and women. It's making our goal of unity – for God's people to be one – seem more and more impossible.

Chapter 1 revealed heart attitudes and bitterness that keep men from having a true Christian understanding that is life changing. Falling back on generational attitudes that inherently teach men to disrespect and disregard women are not those that Christ desires any of us to have. Harboring and exhibiting bitterness toward women – or individuals of any gender – will keep a man from being a servant. If we want to aspire for men to grow as servants of God, then we must look at just what the church is teaching men about themselves, and how that is harmful to their self-image.

Perhaps more so than when this book was first written, an examination of "Alpha Male" Syndrome is in order. If we are top, first, primary, and head, that means Christ is somewhere in our lives, but He is not in the primary place. As Christians, Christ should always be our leader, thus indicating we follow Him, not ourselves. With trends increasing toward male dominance, we are forgetting important principles of humility.

Toxic masculinity

When I wrote the first edition of this book, the term "alpha male" was very common. Today, most would be more familiar with the term "toxic masculinity," which describes the origin of alpha male thinking. Without belaboring this social construct, toxic masculinity is a group of beliefs, ideals, and behaviors used to exaggerate masculine ideals. It's the idea that "manliness" equates to aggression, control, dominance, power, hostility, homophobia, and anti-femininity. It's important to note that toxic masculinity is not saying that all masculine behaviors are toxic, nor is it saying it's bad to be a man or to be masculine. Likewise, no one is nullifying the fact that femininity can also be used for a toxic end, as can anything related to gender stereotyping. If I was to define toxic masculinity, I would say it uses stereotypically masculine traits to the extreme for the end of one's agenda. In other words, when a man behaves in a fashion characteristic to toxic masculinity, they are using their gender to get their own way.

Toxic masculinity is part of social expectation, media and advertising, family dysfunction, and perhaps most relevant in modern times, social media. Male social media influencers – with nothing more than fame and fortune on their minds – take to social media reels and videos creating a narrative where women are endlessly manipulative, trying to steal the male role in society, taking jobs, and rejecting men. In the hands of a man who has recently been burned on dating apps or overlooked on jobs, toxic masculinity can sound like a viable answer. Instead of dealing with the feelings of rejection (that, for the record, men have imposed on women for centuries) or seeking to better themselves, a change among gender social status has many men gravitating toward ideals that are less than healthy.

"Alpha males"

A not-so-subtle message of toxic masculinity is the need for men to be on top, becoming what's known as an "alpha male." An "alpha male" is a man who believes that he should be perpetually in charge, taking the lead in every situation. This includes every sphere of life: at home, in relationships, at work, and in social and religious settings. When I looked up the different characteristics of an alpha male online, there was one word that came up time and time again on every site, and that word is dominance. An alpha male is the man who must be in control of every situation, the "leader of the pack" so to speak. The result: if he is in charge, everyone in his life is properly under his control and follows in tow.

When I explain alpha male identity like this, it doesn't sound very appealing. In fact, it sounds rather abusive. It sounds like a man who must, at all times, have complete control over his environment…including the people in it. It sounds like a recipe for trouble, a man who can turn into something else, at any given time.

Toxic masculinity lauds the alpha male. It makes him sound like the ultimate man, the one everyone wants to be. According to their logic, women love an alpha male and are waiting for a man with these characteristics. The reason I point out the alpha male connection to abuse is because we don't connect the dots ourselves. Rather than creating men who are good husbands, fathers, and considerate of others, we are encouraging our men to become abusers. If we listen to male preachers, teachers, leaders, and authors, the ideal Christian man is an alpha male: emotionless, controlling, dominating, keeping his wife and children in a certain place beneath him, and demanding their complete and unconditional support. It's not cute, it's not funny, and it has turned into a complete recipe for disaster. To think this ridiculous interpretation of the Bible is accurate, we are hurting marriages, families, our witness to various communities, and yes, even men, even if they don't realize it.

Alpha male ideals

There are three main ideals that pertain to the alpha male. They are persistence, male privilege, and male competition.

- **Persistence:** Also related to drive and ambition, men are encouraged to aspire to be the best at everything, even if they aren't good at it. They are encouraged to be over-achievers, driven to do more, be more, and accomplish more.

  There is nothing wrong with encouraging people to follow their dreams or to be the best at whatever it is they seek to do, whether it is in the workplace, at home, or in church. In and of itself, ambition and a drive to be ambitious are not negative, and there is no question that there are many men who can benefit from the encouragement to pursue goals or achieve things in life. The problem with persistence in the alpha male ideal is that persistence in alpha male syndrome is far more than just trying to be the best all-around in life. Persistence in alpha males is not about being a balanced or successful person, but about getting one's way, and believing they should get their way because as a male, they are entitled to such. Rather than being about genuine accomplishment, persistence, drive, and ambition are described as uniquely male qualities that should, therefore, render all men to be precisely on top, always.

In the concept of the alpha male, the word "NO" is not something a man takes very well. His way and his ambition are related to entitlement, and he believes he can have what he always wants if he is persistent and ambitious enough. The alpha male doesn't tend to accept defeat and does not accept that sometimes we have losses in life as well as wins. This can lead to troubling behavior, including mistreatment of others in relationships, a need to be dominant or always feel on top (meaning that others in the relationship are put down), and an intense need and desire for control.

This also causes those with the alpha ideals to feel maligned when they experience rejection in any form. For example, Alpha men tend to blame immigrants, women, and individuals of other genders for their inability to get a job promotion, accepted into a school or other program, or passed up for an opportunity they felt entitled to receive. In the dating realm, rejection from a woman – perhaps finding his behavior inappropriate or offensive or not being interested – also sparks rage and fury, to unhealthy levels. It's easier to blame everyone else or lash out at an unsuspecting individual than it is to say maybe one's behavior is unseemly or, perhaps, maybe this opportunity wasn't right for me at this time.

- **Male privilege:** We've heard a lot about "privilege" in the media the past few years. Some of the things we hear are, I believe, a genuine encouragement for us to see where we stand in society and react accordingly. Some of it, also, is a bit overdone. Privilege is a term to describe the preferential treatment of someone, whether it is rightly earned or not. When we typically hear of it in the media, it is in the context of something that often leads to injustice, because one group has privilege, and therefore, power over another.

There is no question that male privilege is a reality. It has existed for centuries. Men have social relevance over women and those of other genders. It's a fact that men are given more opportunities, jobs, higher pay, better education, and cultural leniency. Court systems expect women to care for children, while men are to provide financially (if they can find them). "Good ol' boy" systems remain a reality. It is, unfortunately, part of the world in which we live.

Alpha male ideals teach male privilege in its varied forms. Men are taught to be literal leaders in every arena of life. As both an expectation and indoctrination, women are to not only need, but also want, men to take the lead in life and stand as the leaders of women. They are taught to be final authorities, decision makers, disciplinarians, and those who take charge of every situation in life. Along with this goes a certain level of entitlement and privilege. For example, most men who believe themselves to be leaders believe they should receive a certain type of treatment as the "head" of any situation. As a result, those around them are subordinate. They expect their subordinates to respond in a certain way, especially women. This way varies, but it revolves around a belief that men have needs, and those in their environment exist to meet them. Whether those needs are cooking and cleaning, child-bearing and raising, sex, or practical subordination in every sense of the term (including sometimes generating income for the benefit of the male), those needs are to be met. The bottom line of male privilege is simple: men are seen as being on top, and women are seen as being on the bottom.

The result of male privilege is what we might now define as "rape culture." Yes, rape culture is the extreme of male privilege, but it is the message that men are not accountable for their behavior. In rape culture, violation of women is normalized because men are seen as superior to all other genders. Even though a small percentage of men are rapists, rape culture starts long before a woman is raped. It exists in a basic concept of inequality: that men have an entitlement to women, and that entitlement can take varied forms, including physical, mental, emotional, or sexual abuse. While rape might only be one example of this, the concept that a woman is a man's property to be taken advantage of is the basic nature and ideal behind rape culture.

- **Male competition:** We've all met men who were brutish, given to fighting and arguments. To a certain extent, we've also met men who are more subtly brutish, on a level we might classify as obnoxious. There was always that one guy someone knew that seemed like he was always ready for a fight. He was jealous over his girlfriend, always fighting with other guys, and always had to outdo everyone else. This guy was one that we all thought to stay away from.

Re-package this guy in terms as jealous over his wife, always trying to outdo other men, and trying to get attention, and you have the perfect image of an alpha male. Competition is often not something that we give much thought to, at least not in a practical sense. With the alpha male ideals, however, male competition becomes a more relevant factor than it might be in an ordinary situation. Alpha men don't just think they are better than women or other genders, they also take on the image that they are better than other men. The competitive nature of the alpha male causes men to look down on one another, especially if a man is not considered to be "manly" or is in some way seen as being effeminate.

How alpha male ideals are taught

Have you ever been present at a men's conference or men's meeting? Most of the time, a woman will send a man to one of those events thinking that it will improve their relationship. She hopes he will gain positive attributes: ones that will help him better care about and relate to her. After all, the church is feminine by nature, and Jesus Himself is a great listener. They think they are sending their men to church, so how could the message they receive be bad?

If women only knew.

It is amazing the kind of words, propaganda, and ideas taught in churches when women are not present. Alpha male ideals are taught in many men's conferences, meetings, books, sermons, and through "buddy systems" supposedly about accountability (they are actually personalized cheerleading sections to keep men immersed in alpha male principles).

The messages seem simple enough: they are disguised as advice or teaching to help men become better husbands and fathers. Most especially, they are packaged as motivation to help a man become the best he can be. Then the teachings start encouraging them to be leaders, because they believe all men are leaders. It then moves to the messages of leading in the home, because women are incapable of handling household matters alongside their

husbands. Children are to be corporally disciplined. They are to be rulers, providers, and make sure everyone around them lines up. The following verses are used to encourage alpha male concepts, perverting their message and introducing a cultural viewpoint to their interpretation:
Proverbs 13:24:

Whoever spares the rod hates their children,
    but the one who loves their children is careful to discipline them.

Proverbs 23:24:

Thou shalt beat him with the rod, and shalt deliver his soul from hell. (KJV)

Ephesians 5:22-24:

Wives, submit yourselves to your own husbands, as you do to the Lord. For the husband is the head of the wife as Christ is the head of the church, His body, of which He is the Savior. Now as the church submits to Christ, so also wives should submit to their husbands in everything.

1 Peter 3:1-7:

Wives, in the same way submit yourselves to your own husbands so that, if any of them do not believe the word, they may be won over without words by the behavior of their wives, when they see the purity and reverence of your lives. Your beauty should not come from outward adornment, such as elaborate hairstyles and the wearing of gold jewelry or fine clothes. Rather, it should be that of your inner self, the unfading beauty of a gentle and quiet spirit, which is of great worth in God's sight. For this is the way the holy women of the past who put their hope in God used to adorn themselves. They submitted themselves to their own husbands, like Sarah, who obeyed Abraham and called him her lord. You are her daughters if you do what is right and do not give way to fear.

Husbands, in the same way be considerate as you live with your wives, and treat them with respect as the weaker partner...

I don't think it's bad to encourage men. I also don't think it's wrong to support men as they step up to be good husbands, fathers, and providers. I think the issue is how we define a good husband, father, and provider. Many of the alpha males I have met don't anywhere meet the definition of what we consider a good husband, father, or provider. Many are ambitious but have bad habits, such as not finishing projects or taking on too many goals. They take on new ideas and positions to the neglect of their families. They often don't discuss what they want to do with their wives and take the finances to do it without considering what will happen to everyone else. They don't spend a lot of time with their children or their wives, unless it is to create a new list of demands. In the effort to create an ideal man, our alpha males often fall short.

How alpha male mentality hurts men

Why do so many men fail when it comes to alpha male aspirations? They believe they are Biblical, and what God desires for them, so they pursue them. However, the average man doesn't meet the criteria to be an alpha male in the truest sense of the term. Most men are average men who desire to be good at what they do and encouraged in who they are. They have varying degrees of sensitivity and attentiveness. Somewhere inside, they desire to be better husbands and fathers and understand their wives and their children. There are also those who truly desire to connect better with God, to become better men in general. So, imagine going to church and suddenly hear that your efforts to try and do all these things: spend time with your kids, love your wife, be considerate of her feelings, and embrace being a family man...are all wrong.

Micah 6:8:

He has shown you, O mortal, what is good.
And what does the LORD require of you?
To act justly and to love mercy
and to walk humbly with your God.

We often hear the blame game: women are the reason men don't want to come to church. Churches that allow women to preach or minister are considered too feminine, and people say everything those women do is wrong, from the colors they paint the wall to the potpourri they use in the bathroom. Have we ever considered that maybe men don't always want to come to church because they are always told they are doing something wrong? The alpha male mentality is something no man can ever live up to in totality, thus causing men to feel inadequate in the eyes of God.

It's not that God doesn't love, nor accepts these men. These men are trying to live up to a standard set by other men. They are seeking identity and relevance, and trying to emulate an idea of masculinity presented as a Biblical ideal. It's a faith by works argument, but no one hears it for what it is. Exposure to something like this long enough makes one feel inadequate. It's not women keeping men from church; it's other men.

It's also important to consider the way alpha male mentality hurts marriages. Over time, women desire their husbands to grow to know them. It's a wife's hope her husband will consider her thoughts and feelings about problems and situations rather than rushing in to make rash decisions. If a man consistently tells a woman what to do or makes decisions that affect her without considering her feelings or asking what she thinks, she will feel like she has no relevance in his life. Women do not desire to be led. They desire to be in a partnership with someone they know cares about them. This type of relationship building block, where spouses are both free to talk in their marriages, doesn't come from a man always off and running in different directions. Making demands of a wife or children doesn't create communication. Just as with the many complaints women tend to have about men, men need to learn how to listen and be attentive others in their lives. Maybe more than anything, this consideration of others is something that desperately needs to be taught.

As an example: The show *Sister Wives* depicts the demise of a polygamous family over a period of about 20 years. Several years ago, there was an episode where patriarch Kody goes to Texas for his anniversary with now divorced wife, Christine. They also went along with their therapist, who went to help them with some of their issues. As of this episode, they were married 21 years. Even then, they had severe intimacy and communication issues. These issues were further compounded by their complicated home life, involving many children, three other wives, and a complicated Mormon Fundamentalist belief system.

As part of an exercise in communication, Kody and Christine were instructed by their therapist to go to the beach and create a rock wall that symbolized their relationship. Through the entire event, Kody steamrolled everything Christine said, thought, and any suggestions she had. He wanted to focus on the bigger family unit, but she wanted the wall to represent their love and commitment to each other. She didn't want everything to be about the family all the time. After a frustrating and exhaustive experience, both met with the therapist and stated more of their needs. It was obvious they didn't come to a better understanding of one another or what their needs were. They both gained some insight into their different priorities, but they were unable to find ways to meet in the middle and resolve their issues. The reason? Their religion teaches the man's perspective is higher than the woman's, and that makes compromise impossible.

If you follow this show, you know Kody and Christine are now divorced. Kody is also divorced from two other wives, Jenelle and Meri. While he remains married now, as a monogamous man, to Robyn, some question the stability of that relationship, as well. The past few seasons have been full of rants that make it clear Kody had certain ideas about himself as a man that these women did not support. The more he asserted himself as an "alpha male," the more he drove the women in his life away.

Most alpha men are monogamous, not polygamous, as was the situation on *Sister Wives*. The Fundamentalist Mormon mentality, however, creates a clear picture of the toxic alpha male-female dynamic. Because members of Mormon Fundamentalism are encouraged to have large families as a part of their theological understanding, it is understandable to think a family with nearly 20 children and multiple adults needs some sort of structure and leadership. Yet in these situations, everything requires a group mentality: the family, the co-op of marriages, and the needs of everyone versus the needs of the one or the couple. In every situation, the family swallows up the individual and the couple. The family is a big pack, with one head leader. There is no consideration for change or identity, for feelings or for compromise, because the environment is always primed for chaos. There are simply too many children and adults in that one generation within one family.

Christine, a wife, was looking for her husband, Kody. She was often quoted at the beginning of the show to state "I wanted a family, not just the man," and that is why she joined this family. Now, down the line, she's at a different place in her life. Her children are getting older. As they start to leave home and her life change, she now wants the man more than the family. She wants her husband to talk to her, communicate with her, engage with her, and love her. According to his religion, he was never taught how to do this. He knows how to lead, he knows how to make decisions and exert a sense of being in charge, but he has never learned how to love his wife or to affirm her as a person.

This is an example of what alpha male mentality does to a marriage. A husband gets so caught up in the concept of leadership that he forgets there are certain human needs and connections far more essential to develop in a marriage. When a marriage becomes all about a family and not at all about a couple, or all about one partner and never about the other, the basic balance of a marriage is lost. In such a situation, spouses are unable to connect with one another in a way that transcends life changes.

The way that alpha male church confuses men

If you think about the messages we receive in church, they are, overall, often confusing. We hear slogans and sayings, but we don't hear much teaching. We are told "we're the head and not the tail," but then we are told to remain humble. We're told to be bold, but then we are told we need to be cautious. We're told not to be superstitious and then cautioned against spirits being attached to inanimate objects. We're told we shouldn't be greedy, but then encouraged to aspire for things we don't need, such as bigger houses and cars. Then we are told we should do for or share with others, but as a church, we never are given the opportunity to do so or told just how to do it.

These are just a sample of the contradictory messages we receive. We receive them for one simple reason: Most churches have stopped requiring clergy education and instead gravitate toward those who are the most entertaining in the pulpit. We don't uphold standards of understanding on Scriptural and ministerial matters. As a result, we have an entire generation of leadership that takes their lead from popular preachers, authors, and Christian Hollywood, all teaching without proper understanding. They are leading us, quite honestly, into a spiritual ditch.

2 Samuel 12:15-23:

After Nathan had gone home, the LORD struck the child that Uriah's wife had borne to David, and he became ill. David pleaded with God for the child. He fasted and spent the nights lying in sackcloth on the ground. The elders of his household stood beside him to get him up from the ground, but he refused, and he would not eat any food with them.

On the seventh day the child died. David's attendants were afraid to tell him that the child was dead, for they thought, "While the child was still living, he wouldn't listen to us when we spoke to him. How can we now tell him the child is dead? He may do something desperate."

David noticed that his attendants were whispering among themselves, and he realized the child was dead. "Is the child dead?" he asked.

"Yes," they replied, "he is dead."

Then David got up from the ground. After he had washed, put on lotions and changed his clothes, he went into the house of the LORD and worshiped. Then he went to his own house, and at his request they served him food, and he ate.

His attendants asked him, "Why are you acting this way? While the child was alive, you fasted and wept, but now that the child is dead, you get up and eat!"

He answered, "While the child was still alive, I fasted and wept. I thought, "Who knows?" The LORD may be gracious to me and let the child live. But now that the is dead, why should I go on fasting? Can I bring him back again? I will go to him, but he will not return to me."

1 Kings 11:1-8:

King Solomon, however, loved many foreign women besides Pharaoh's daughter – Moabites, Ammonites, Edomites, Sidonians and Hittites. They were from nations about which the LORD had told the Israelites, "You must not intermarry with them, because they will surely turn your hearts after their gods." Nevertheless, Solomon held fast to them in love. He had seven hundred wives of royal birth and three hundred concubines, and his wives led him astray. As Solomon grew old, his wives turned his heart after other gods, and his heart was not fully devoted to the LORD his God, as the heart of David his father had been. He followed Ashtoreth the goddess of the Sidonians, and Molek the detestable god of the Ammonites. So Solomon did evil in the eyes of the LORD; he did not follow the LORD completely, as David his father had done.

On a hill east of Jerusalem, Solomon built a high place for Chemosh the detestable god of Moab, and for Molek the detestable god of the Ammonites. He did the same for all his foreign wives, who burned incense and offered sacrifices to their gods.

Nehemiah 13:26:

Did not Solomon king of Israel sin by these things? yet among many nations was there no king like him, who was beloved of his God, and God made him king over all Israel: nevertheless even him did outlandish women cause to sin. (KJV)

I meet many men who read the Bible on their own and wind up even more confused when it comes to what they learn about women at church. Alpha male teaching confuses men because the characteristics of the alpha male are in direct contrast to the characteristics they often see in men in the Bible. Men such as Solomon, who had many wives, were punished for that fact. He was disciplined by God because his many pagan wives led him into idolatry, according to the account. But have we ever considered that part of that idolatry was having so many women in his life, and not being able to properly attend to or care for them as individuals? David, who committed the ultimate alpha male sin by raping Bathsheba and having her husband killed, also reaped the ultimate consequence for what he did. Time and time again, the behaviors of dominance, control, male privilege, and male superiority didn't go over well with God.

Men can read the Bible and get the message that God expects them to put aside the characteristics they often exercise and adapt as a part of worldly behaviors and put on the new nature that is Christ-like. Christ's character was peaceful, calm, quiet, and commanding without having to use physical violence, force, demean other people, put others down, or over-achieve. Jesus was the ultimate success just by being Himself. He was in no way what we would define today as an "alpha male."

We can't expect men to stay somewhere where they feel confused and unsupported. There is no such thing as a "men's role" in the Bible. Being a man is not a Biblical role; it is a worldly concept. There isn't just one way to be a man in the Bible, either. There are various sides of different men exposed from a Biblical perspective: we see male poets, musicians, prophets, writers, leaders, intercessors, lovers, thinkers, warriors, husbands, and yes, even fathers. We see Biblical males as real people, not idealized characters. They had their ups and downs, flaws, successes, and one great commonality: they all sought to become better servants of God, even if they didn't always understand how to do that.

Why Biblical characteristics are so relevant to men

I personally love the writings of the Apostles Peter and Paul. It is obvious to me they struggled deeply with themselves not just as leaders, but as men. The Apostle John, who we often call the "love apostle," had a special and unique understanding of Who Jesus was and his own insights into spiritual things. Based on his writings, we would, most likely, classify him as more sensitive and perceptive. I don't get this sense from the Apostles Peter and Paul. We know from the Gospel accounts that Peter was a zealot, and tended to react with drama, violence and anger when he was riled. Paul was known for having Christians killed and for his punitive nature pre-salvation. When both came to receive the Lord in their lives in a way that moved them to greater things, both knew how important it was to change their nature. Rather than living in a brutish, fleshly way, they were called to lay down themselves and take up the nature of Christ.

1 Peter 2:1-3:

So then, rid yourselves of all evil, all lying [deceit], hypocrisy, jealousy [envy], and evil speech [slander; all traits that destroy relationships; Rom. 13:13; Eph. 4:25–32; Col. 3:8]. As newborn babies want milk, you should want the pure [sincere; unadulterated] and simple [or spiritual] teaching [milk; probably referring to the word of God; see 1:23–25]. By it you can mature [grow; reach maturity] in your salvation, because you have already examined and seen [tasted] how good the Lord is [Ps. 34:8]. (EXB)

1 Corinthians 13:1-3:

I may speak in different languages [tongues; 12:10, 29, 30] of people or even angels. But if I do not have love, I am only a noisy [resounding] bell [gong] or a crashing [clanging] cymbal. I may have the gift of prophecy. I may understand all the secret things of God [mysteries] and have all knowledge, and I may have faith so great I can move mountains. But even with all these things, if I do not have love, then I am nothing. I may give away everything I have, and I may even give my body as an offering to be burned [to be burned]. But I gain nothing if I do not have love. (EXB)

It's hard to believe these passages were written by men who, at one point in time, would have been classified as "alpha men." There is one very important explanation for their turnaround: they finally came to a place where they recognized they were called to be servants. They stepped back to understand the Scriptures in light of that concept, rather than trying to use the Scriptures to further their own vein fleshly understandings of themselves.

In addition to recognizing Scripture, they also examined their leadership considering Christ's example. Jesus didn't conquer the world by violence, but by an act of love that is unfathomable to us, even today. He committed no sin and did no wrong and still received a punishment that wasn't for Him. He did this for the salvation of the world – for the betterment of others. It wasn't about being top dog or in charge but leading as a servant. Rather than entitlement, Jesus emptied Himself so much, the early apostles couldn't fathom but be changed. If Jesus, being in the form of God could assume human flesh to live, walk, teach, and then suffer and die for our sins, surely they could set aside their egotistical need to be on top and in charge and assume a new way of leading others.

These men – and countless others – recognized God was the Alpha, not them.

The fact that much of the Bible was written by men and was written from the viewpoint of men should tell us something about the characteristics male believers should have. They expressed emotions: sorrow, grief, overwhelm, fear, joy, excitement, anger, hope, happiness, gladness, and beyond. The call for love, compassion, understanding, forgiveness, right speech, and right attitudes are things not exclusive to women or individuals of other genders. Bible advice isn't for everyone except men. It isn't any more understandable for a man to refrain from doing these things because he is a man. If anything, it becomes less understandable.

Rather than pushing men to adopt a worldly understanding of manliness, men's ministries should instruct men in true Biblical character. They should be taught to be more like Christ, not like the world. Every man should aspire to be like their Savior, treating others as He would treat them, and holding all things together with love, rather than control. He, as is every Christian man, called to be a servant: to his wife, to his children, and to his community.

Reflections

- Do you fit in with church teaching directed towards men? Why or why not?

- How do you feel about church teaching toward men? Do you find anything about it confusing? If so, what?

- What kind of character do you feel is appropriate for a Christian man?

3
BECOMING SOMEBODY
MEANS SERVING SOMEBODY

————————————=( )=————————————

AND IF IT SEEM EVIL UNTO YOU TO SERVE THE LORD, CHOOSE YOU THIS DAY
WHOM YE WILL SERVE; WHETHER THE GODS WHICH YOUR FATHERS SERVED
THAT WERE ON THE OTHER SIDE OF THE FLOOD, OR THE GODS OF THE AMORITES,
IN WHOSE LAND YE DWELL: BUT AS FOR ME AND MY HOUSE, WE WILL SERVE THE LORD.
(JOSHUA 24:15, KJV)

- **Reading assignment:** The Book of Philippians

Years ago, Bob Dylan sang the words, "It may be the devil, or it may be the Lord, but you're gonna have to serve somebody." Whether you are a Dylan fan or not, you can't argue the truth of that statement. No matter what our interests are, how mighty or powerful we might act, how much money we have, or how great we think we are, we have to serve somebody. Even though we don't get many choices as to what we do all the time, this is one of those areas where we get to decide. Who we choose to serve is our choice. We can either serve the devil, we can try to serve men to win favor or get ahead (which probably won't work), or we can serve the Lord. The choice is ours, and the decision we make impacts everything else that comes along in our lives.

Choosing who we serve changes our perspectives on servanthood. One of the primary messages that alpha male teachings convey is that men shouldn't serve but be served. This is against every Biblical principle in existence. If you call yourself a follower of God and a lover of Christ, then that means you should be a servant, regardless of gender.

Most people balk at the idea of service. It is considered demeaning to serve others, whether for money or the Kingdom (even nowadays). Society regards those in service-based industries (such as food service, housekeeping, or retail) as being among the lowest of low workers in our country. People give orders as part of their jobs are regarded as highly prestigious. Those who must take those orders may face intimidation or abusive treatment. We like the idea of living a lifestyle of the rich and famous, where other people serve us, and we don't have to serve anyone.

Servanthood seems difficult for many men, for all the reasons we have discussed throughout this book. Men are taught that service is demeaning and beneath them, something for women, girls, other genders, and poor people to do. When it comes to housework, dinner, meals, childcare, and life, many men still expect those duties to defer to women. Considering modern culture and attitudes about wealth and prosperity, being a servant sounds like something for someone else...maybe anyone else.

Men are called to be servants, just like everyone else. In fact, many of the passages in the Bible that address servanthood were addressed to crowds of men or to men who tried to skirt around the issue for much of their lives. They were looking for someone to elevate their status and make them top dog, top of the food chain, someone to whom the world bowed down to, honored, and adored.

This isn't what God expects, nor asks, of us. God asks us to lay ourselves down for others, in love and sacrifice. It's a hard job, but somebody's got to do it! In terms of our faith, it takes a true Christian, confident in what God has called them to be, empowered enough by the Spirit to be a servant to others, always.

What does "being somebody" mean to you?

1 Peter 2:5:

You come to Him as living stones, a spiritual house that is being built into a holy priesthood. So offer spiritual sacrifices that God accepts through Jesus Christ. (GW)

When I was in sixth grade, we were asked to do a class essay on where we aspired to be by the time we turned 30 (wow, if I even had a clue). Almost all of us talked about wanting to have a lot of money and be famous. Our principal, Sr. Maureen, sat in the back of the room and observed. After listening for awhile, she said to us, "You all talk about having money like that's going to make somebody happy. There are many millionaires out there who are miserable."

If we're listening in today's church, you wouldn't know this. It seems like every miracle, message, new start, and new adventure this side of heaven revolves around money. We're definitely given the message that money will make us who we aspire to be. If we believe any of these people are really hearing from God, one will think God espouses worldly ideas: He wants us all to be rich, famous, and "relevant" in a trendy, worldly sense. There are many who even teach that spiritual leaders should be at the forefront of secular business and culture, and that we should all aspire to "be somebody."

Aspiration, aspiration, aspiration!!!!

Truth is that alpha male attitudes have translated into alpha people Christianity. All those ambitions, attitudes, dominances, and master of our domain concepts that we teach men underline the very face of Christianity as we understand it today. No matter how much we try to deflect it in clothing that looks like we just mowed the lawn or those graphic-print button-down shirts I despise, the push to be or do or be better than the world drives Christians today. We think aspiration is the secret to everything, and we should always do and be the best. In this push, we eliminate very key portions of the Gospel message, including important attitudes we should espouse. Every one of these relates to service and our call to serve others.

I've heard it said from the pulpit that "everybody wants to be somebody; nobody wants to be a nobody." I'd say that's a true statement, but there is something key the statement is missing. What it means to be "somebody" is different for all people and often changes in people's lives. What I wish I'd heard more of in church was just how true what my principal said to us in that sixth-grade classroom over thirty years ago. Just because people are rich, famous, or successful according to someone's definition doesn't mean someone is relevant, or happy, or has purpose in life. They might be good at looking and sounding the part, but it's obvious that what defines us as somebody in someone's life isn't money, nor fame, nor any of the stuff society sends us on a wild hunt to find. Even though having all the money and attention in the world might be great, it is obviously not, at the end of the day, what matters to most people. We're missing the boat with being "somebody" because we are looking for it in all the wrong places.

So where does it lie? If we're being lied to about what it means to be somebody great, what is the truth about being great? How can we be great? What is the secret of being great?

Jesus gave us the answer, many of us just don't like what it is.

Matthew 20:20-28:

Then the mother of Zebedee's sons came to Jesus with her sons and, kneeling down, asked a favor of Him.

"What is it you want?" He asked.

She said, "Grant that one of these two sons of mine may sit at Your right and the other at Your left in your kingdom."

"You don't know what you are asking," Jesus said to them. "Can you drink the cup I am going to drink?"

"We can," they answered.

Jesus said to them, "You will indeed drink from My cup, but to sit at My right or left is not for me to grant. These places belong to those for whom they have been prepared by My Father."

When the ten heard about this, they were indignant with the two brothers. Jesus called them together and said, "You know that the rulers of the Gentiles lord it over them, and their high officials exercise authority over them. Not so with you. Instead, whoever wants to become great among you must be your servant, and whoever wants to be first must be your slave— just as the Son of Man did not come to be served, but to serve, and to give His life as a ransom for many."

Matthew 25:34-40:

"Then the King will say to those on His right, 'Come, you who are blessed by My Father; take your inheritance, the kingdom prepared for you since the creation of the world. For I was hungry and you gave Me something to eat, I was thirsty and you gave Me something to drink, I was a stranger and you invited Me in, I needed clothes and you clothed Me, I was sick and you looked after Me, I was in prison and you came to visit Me.'

"Then the righteous will answer Him, 'Lord, when did we see You hungry and feed You, or thirsty and give You something to drink? When did we see You a stranger and invite You in, or needing clothes and clothe You? When did we see You sick or in prison and go to visit You?'

"The King will reply, 'Truly I tell you, whatever you did for one of the least of these brothers and sisters of Mine, you did for Me.'

If you want to be somebody, you've got to serve somebody.

It's as simple as that. All the things we chase, hoping they will make us somebody, are not things that, when it comes down to it, will matter.

The Bible doesn't make serving easy, however. It doesn't just tell us to serve those we like, or who we are closest to, or whoever is most convenient. We are told that we need to serve:

- **All**: Every person we encounter. We talk about serving leaders or other Christians, but sorry folks, Christians are supposed to be serving everyone, both believers and non-believers alike. It is true that sometimes God gives assignments to serve in a specific way, but our attitude of servanthood should extend to anyone and everyone, at any time.

- **The "least" of these**: In Biblical times, the least of these was a financial distinction meant to indicate someone was considered poor or socially irrelevant. This status typically went to women, children, the sick, and beggars. More specifically, it refers to someone who can't return the favor back (you are giving to give because you know they can't return the favor). In more modern understanding, it represents anyone we regard with a certain level of disdain or contempt. If you feel superior to someone else because they can't do anything "useful" for you, you have discovered your "least." That's who you should get busy serving.

- **Leaders in the Kingdom**: Kingdom leaders are servants and that means they always bear the responsibility of service. From our leaders, we should learn service. In response, we should rise up to serve them, too! Being of service to a leader doesn't mean becoming their personal slave, but that we should be eager to assist in the expansion of the Kingdom with our finances, time, support, and assistance. Leaders should not have to twist anyone's arm to get help with ministry work.

- **Our elders**: The Bible reiterates the need to respect those who are older than us, especially parents, grandparents, and those who have gone before us in the faith. It doesn't mean we do things the way they always did them or fall behind with excuses to avoid change, but it does mean we respect that our ancestors paved the way for us to be where we are now. We honor their contributions to our lives, our faith, and the place we are, right now.

- **Each other**: The Scriptures emphasize that, as Christians, we should be willing to serve one another. Even though there may be people in church we don't like or won't want to connect with as social friends, we should always be ready, willing, and able to extend a helping hand in service to our siblings in Christ.

It's obvious that servanthood is an important thing in the life of a Christian, no matter how we view it. It's something we need to learn about. More than anything else, we must take it seriously. We should never, ever brush off service as someone else's job, something that somebody else should do for us, or something that isn't our concern or interest. If anything, service should be of primary concern for everyone in church, from the leaders on down, and should be a topic we hear about on a regular basis. It is a topic that is THAT important.

<u>Servanthood in Bible times</u>

Leviticus 25:39:

If an Israelite becomes poor and sells himself to you, don't work him like a slave. (GW)

Exodus 22:3:

A thief must make up for what he has stolen. If he is unable to do so, he must be sold as a slave to pay for what he stole. (GW)

2 Kings 4:1:

One of the wives of a disciple of the prophets called to Elisha, "Sir, my husband is dead! You know how he feared the LORD. Now a creditor has come to take my two children as slaves." (GW)

One of the reasons we aren't up on service like we should be is because we don't understand it. Certainly, it's not the most fun topic a preacher could pick for a Sunday morning sermon. People would rather scour the Bible with fervor over something like prosperity or wealth rather than learn about serving others. As a result, I think we hear that we are supposed to "serve," but we fast-forward over it to something else that sounds more enticing. We don't pay enough attention to it for it to sink in and change our lives....so that means we don't know what it means to dive in and do it.

Skipping over servanthood in favor of other topics deemed more fun or interesting is not an excuse for not serving. There comes a point where we all must accept that the Scriptures aren't about pleasing or accommodating us, but an entire expanse of understanding for our growth and development. Thus, I think before we start looking at specific examples of servanthood in the Bible (which we will do in the following chapters), it is best to look at what being a "servant" meant in Bible times.

In ancient cultures, servants were considered the lowest of the low because they had to do servile work. Servanthood was associated with slavery or very low-paying jobs, as work nobody wanted to do. In fact, the Biblical word for "servant" is often "slave," as both were associated as being one and the same.

That's not to say that servants weren't prized for their

work. Servants and slaves were considered an important part of ancient economies (especially among Greece and Rome), as their skills contributed valuable labor to society. Though enslaved, they were regarded as participants within ancient culture. This isn't to say they were treated well (there are instances of abuse and mistreatment) or that slavery was a good or just thing, but that within ancient culture, its perception was a little different than its modern context. There are different reasons why someone might have been a slave (we will discuss this next), and different skills afforded different "levels," if you will, of slavery. Slaves could be doctors, artisans, teach children, work in physical or farm labor, household duties, or executive positions, where they served the king or other government officials.

There are a few reasons why someone might have been a slave in ancient society. The most common reason was economics, whereby an individual owed a debt to someone else. Too pay off that debt, they offered themselves in service. The master would then look after that individual, and the slave or servant would work as their own personal property. After so many years, many servants were classified as free to go, but many chose to stay on with their owners, as servants were often considered trusted individuals, especially if their service was out of a life-long commitment or obligation.

Other reasons for servanthood include prisoners of war, children sold into slavery to pay off a debt, inherited servanthood (such as a slave left in a will to a family), and in a less glamorous turn of events, there were slaves who were criminals. There are many examples of servanthood and slavery in the Bible. Even though we often associate servanthood with menial positions (and those in the Bible did, as well), not all the positions of a servant were, as we can see above, the literal bottom of the barrel. This having been said, when Jesus gave His personal example of servanthood, He did a job considered the most menial of all tasks.

John 13:1-17:

It was almost time for [Now before...,] the Passover Feast [12:12]. Jesus knew that it was time [the hour] for Him to leave [depart from] this world and go back to the Father. He had always loved those who were His own in the world, and he loved them all the way to the end [or completely; totally].

Jesus and His followers were at the evening meal [It was dinnertime]. The devil had already persuaded [put it into the heart of] Judas Iscariot, the son of Simon, to turn against [betray] Jesus. Jesus knew that the Father had given Him power over everything [placed everything into His hands] and that He had come from God and was going back to God. So during the meal [from supper] Jesus stood up and took off His outer clothing. Taking a towel, He wrapped it around His waist. Then He poured water into a bowl and began to wash the followers' [disciples'] feet, drying [wiping] them with the towel that was wrapped around Him. [This act was considered so demeaning by some people that they only allowed Gentile slaves to do it.]

Jesus came to Simon Peter, who said to Him, "Lord, are You going to wash my feet?"

Jesus answered, "You don't understand now what I am doing, but you will understand later."

Peter said, "No, You will never wash my feet."

Jesus answered, "If I don't wash your feet, you are not one of My people [have no share/part with Me]."

Simon Peter answered, "Lord, then wash not only my feet, but wash my hands and my head, too!"

Jesus said to Him, "After a person has had a bath [washed; bathed], his whole body is clean. He needs only to wash his feet. And you men are clean, but not all of you." [For] Jesus knew who would turn against [betray] Him, and that is why He said, "Not all of you are clean."

When He had finished washing their feet, He put on his clothes and sat down [reclined; the posture for a banquet or dinner party] again. He asked, "Do you understand what I have just done for [to] you? You call me 'Teacher' and 'Lord' [titles appropriately ascribed to an esteemed Rabbi, but which took on deeper meaning after His death and resurrection], and you are right, because that is what I am. If I, your Lord and Teacher, have washed your feet, you also should wash each other's feet. I did this as an example [a pattern] so that you should do as I have done for you. I tell you the truth [Truly, truly, I say to you], a servant [slave; bond-servant] is not greater than his master [lord]. [And] A messenger is not greater than the one who sent him. If you know these things, you will be blessed if you do them. (EXB)

Washing feet was a long-standing sign of Middle Eastern hospitality. People wore sandals rather than shoes and did not bathe daily, causing dirty and dusty feet upon entry into a home. It was customary for one to remove their shoes before going inside, and that meant a person would track all sorts of dirt, sand, and dust into a house. People in the Middle Eastern cultures also eat reclining on the floor, which meant that dirty feet in a household could cause contamination, illness, or messiness. A household servant washed the feet of guests, showing honor and respect. Doing it was a big deal. Not doing it was a sign of disrespect, that you didn't want that person in your home.

It was also a job that nobody wanted, which shouldn't come as a big shock. Who in the world wants to wash someone's dirty, nasty feet? Since it wasn't a big, fancy, coveted position, it was considered the most demeaning and menial of tasks. Such was done out of obligation, rather than excitement or honor.

For Jesus to wash His disciples' feet, not only with a good attitude but teaching that we should do it ourselves was a mighty big deal. It probably resulted in shock and horror, with a few whispers all over the room. Sure, Jesus was on the radical side, but telling His disciples to wash feet? That sounded extreme, even for Him. It didn't help that as an occupied people, the Jews of His day already had a negative view of their occupiers, the Romans. They saw them as inferior people. Not only are we dealing with that, we also must be servants and wash feet, too?

Yup. If we aren't washed of Him, we have no part of Him. In other words, if we do not allow ourselves to be touched by Him in our lives, cleansed in baptism, washed in the water of the Word and raised to new life with Him, then we do not have part with Him. If we haven't received His service to us, then we have not really received Him.

Jesus doesn't stop there, though. It isn't enough for us to just receive Him and then go on our merry way. If we have received Him and become a part of Him, He lives in us. If we are to truly partake of Christ and the life He desires us to have, we must model what Jesus did...and serve others.

Peter missed the point when he asked to have his body washed, including his hands and feet. This makes me think of many I've met who constantly seek more spiritual expressions, but don't ever do much with them. They want to experience Jesus, but they don't understand that such spirituality lacks the practicality of Jesus' spiritual walk. I'd imagine many more Christians are also missing this same point. We talk all the time about wanting more of Jesus and being filled in an even greater way with Him, but not about doing the things He did. It's fine to want more of Jesus, but we should do something with our spiritual overflow. We can't say that Jesus lives in us and then not want to do something for others. The two simply do not go together. In the Christian life, it's not enough to want to achieve a deep spiritual state or deep spiritual insights. We won't ever develop the spiritual insights we want to have about God and about His ways if we don't serve.

<u>Updating the concept of a Biblical servant</u>

Foot washing remains a practice in the Middle East,

although now it's mostly associated with religious custom. Since most people don't abide by the practice any longer, where does that leave us today? Are Jesus' words about service just archaic? The answer to these two questions is no, His words are not archaic, and what we do now is find new ways to serve. Whether it's literally washing feet or something else, service is service.

From Jesus' words, we can break down the following about service:

- **We should seek opportunities to be of service:** Many people don't serve because they think whatever they do in service should come to them, thus they don't find it. I have met many who sit around and wait for God to "reveal" to them what kind of service they should do. I don't think it's wrong to seek guidance, but sometimes we must try some things out to discover where we are effective. If we don't seek out service, service will ever find us where we are.

- **We need to approach service with the right mindset:** If we have the wrong attitude about service, we won't find our Savior in it. We must approach service as a part of the whole of the Christian life, as something that teaches us about Jesus, ourselves, life, and our witness.

- **It's not always convenient:** If you are waiting for service to appear at a convenient time, you will never serve. Service is one of those commitments that you must see through, no matter how inconvenient it might be. If you are to do it, then follow it through to the end.

- **It is sometimes menial (at least in the view of the world):** I'm sure Jesus didn't wash the disciples' feet as He whistled a happy tune and thought about how much fun it was. He was doing what needed to be done and teaching the disciples a lesson: no matter how menial the job, the bottom line of service is making sure things get done. A true servant will do whatever is necessary, whether it is cleaning the bathroom, preaching the Gospel, cooking a meal, visiting a shut-in, helping a co-worker, or cleaning a house.

- **What we do does not reflect our status in society, but our status in the Kingdom:** Before God, we all stand humble. That is as true for the greatest king in the land as it is for the homeless man who lives on the street. No job is too big or too small for those who call God their Father to do. It's not about being haughty, but being purposeful.

- **It's not just about soup kitchens and clothing drives (although those are fine forms of service):** Sometimes we stigmatize one form of service as being the only form of service. It's fine to volunteer to run a soup kitchen or a clothing drive, but there are other things that need doing, which also represent Kingdom work. When it comes to service, it's great to be creative. Don't rely on the same stereotyped forms of service all the time.

- **It's not all about being good to your family (although this is fine, too):** Sometimes we over-emphasize family to the point of making family a ministry all its own. This gives the impression you can do outreach right in your own house. Yes, we should be of service to our families and yes, we should witness to our families, but that does not nullify our obligation to reach out to our communities, to others at church, and to people in genuine need. If you are so busy with family commitments that you have no time to do anything else, then you aren't serving like you should.

- **It's not all about what happens at church (although**

church is a great place to serve): It takes everyone to keep our churches functioning. Every member should be involved in at least two helps ministries (we will talk more about this later) to keep church flowing. If you are a part of a church and you aren't serving in it, you need to get involved. Church is often a primary place where we learn about service. Don't think, however, that service only happens at church. Wherever there are people, there are opportunities to serve.

- **It is not something we should judge:** Just because someone serves differently than you doesn't mean their service is less in the eyes of the Lord. Our service is equal in God's eyes, as we do it with the right heart.

- **There will always be an opportunity to be of service, somewhere:** If you can't find anything to do for someone else, you aren't looking hard enough.

Modern Biblical servanthood is being willing to do whatever it takes to get the job done as God leads us to do. It doesn't matter how menial, or unimportant it might seem. It takes our responsibility, commitment, and participation with God to see that all needs are met. Each of us shares the responsibility in this process.

Ways we confuse servanthood for men

I believe that we confuse servanthood for everyone. We all receive the message that service isn't really desirable, and it's not something any of us should want to do. There's a point, however, where the messages we receive differ. We're told that women are designed to serve their families (especially the men in them), whereas men are supposed to provide for their families. Without any context, this fuels the alpha male image we spoke of in the last chapter (which is, in essence, contrary to servanthood). It also gives women the responsibility to over-compensate for what men fail to do. I have met many ridiculously confused families, following the demands of a man who thinks a woman should serve him because he provides money to the household. In the most extreme examples, it's because they are the "men" of the household. I've also met many children in households with very ambitious fathers. They think the best way to make their children proud or acknowledge them is to be successful at work. They believe their wives will take pride in the amount of money they make and see that as compensation for the things they miss. The problem with this is that it isn't what the average person is looking for, at all.

We pump men full of ideas like these, then we talk about servanthood and wonder why there is confusion. Do you think any of these different attitudes and expectations are those Jesus would have in a household setting? If not, why are we pursuing them? The ways of the world are not the ways of God, nor are God's ways worldly ways. Men are not above service, because the Savior of the world, our Immanuel, the Word made flesh Himself, got down with a towel and basin and washed feet because it needed to be done. He didn't go and find a woman to do it for Him or tell the disciples to find women to do the menial tasks and labors that were beneath them. Instead, He told them to get down and do it themselves. In doing so, they would partake of His life, His ministry, His hope, and His heart.

This means that, as a man, if you want a better relationship with Christ, you need to make sure you have a solid understanding of service. You shouldn't be demanding others so they'll recognize how much you want to be served, but how much you should be doing for them. Whether it is at home, at work, at church, or in the community, or as a man, you need to be a doer, rather than a receiver.

Ephesians 5:25-32:

Husbands, love your wives as Christ loved the church [Col. 3:19; 1 Pet. 3:7] and gave Himself for her to make her holy [sanctify her], cleansing her in the washing of water by the word [the "washing" may be (1) baptism, (2) spiritual cleansing (Titus 3:5), or (3) an analogy drawn from the Jewish prenuptial bath (Ezek. 16:8–14); the "word" may be (1) the Gospel, (2) a baptismal formula, or (3) the confession of the one baptized]. He did this so that He could present the church to Himself like a bride in all her beauty [in splendor; glorious], with no evil or sin [stain or wrinkle] or any other wrong thing in it [such thing], but pure [holy] and without fault [blameless]. In the same way, husbands should love their wives as they love their own bodies. The man who loves his wife loves himself. [For] No one ever hates his own body [flesh], but feeds and takes care of it. And that is what Christ does for the church, because we are parts [members] of His body. The Scripture says, "So [For this reason] a man will leave his father and mother and be united [joined] with his wife, and the two will become one body [flesh; Gen. 2:24]." This secret [mystery] is very important [or great; profound]—I am talking about Christ and the church. (EXB)

This is why servanthood is so important for Christian men. We've heard a lot of gripe that the church is becoming too feminine. Since the church herself is a girl (the word for church is feminine in the Greek), the whole concept that the church is too feminine is ridiculous. The problem isn't the church, it's that the church is not doing her job to lead all people to the Lord. Service is an important outlet for men in their connection to Jesus.

We have reduced spiritual outpouring, expression and experience to a few key points that seem to define too much of who we are as believers. If someone doesn't find their experience in one of those few moments, we decide someone's relationship with God is not right. Not so! Not every man (just like not every other person) finds their relational expression in the Lord by standing around, arms raised, hysterical in church during the right worship song. Not every man wants to roll around on the floor in a state of spiritual ecstasy. And yes, not every man wants to sit around and hear teaching about being a man while he and other men in the church are made to listen to the same thing that they already heard a thousand other times.

Servanthood is one of the most powerful ways that men can connect with their Savior. In His human life, Jesus was male. At that, Jesus was also a man Who served, Who was on the front lines of human compassion and concern. If a man can serve, then that is a man who can stand before anyone as a decent human being, as a powerful man of God, and who can walk in the feet of Jesus, experiencing His call, for himself.

Principles of servanthood

One of the smallest – and least-studied – books of the New Testament is the book of Philemon. It is a letter from the Apostle Paul to Philemon, a slave-owner with a runaway slave by the name of Onesimus. The long and the short of this very short story is: Paul urged Philemon to reconcile with Onesimus and for Onesimus to return to Philemon. The testimony of service, and the way Paul urges both men to work out their issues, shines through powerfully in its 25 verses:

This letter is from Paul, a prisoner for preaching the Good News about Christ Jesus, and from our brother Timothy.

I am writing to Philemon, our beloved co-worker, and to our sister Apphia, and to our fellow soldier Archippus, and to the church that meets in your house.

May God our Father and the Lord Jesus Christ give you grace and peace.

I always thank my God when I pray for you, Philemon, because I keep hearing about your faith in the Lord Jesus and your love for all of God's people. And I am praying that you will put into action the generosity that comes from your faith as you understand and experience all the good things we have in Christ. Your love has given me much joy and comfort, my brother, for your kindness has often refreshed the hearts of God's people.

That is why I am boldly asking a favor of you. I could demand it in the name of Christ because it is the right thing for you to do. But because of our love, I prefer simply to ask you. Consider this as a request from me—Paul, an old man and now also a prisoner for the sake of Christ Jesus.

I appeal to you to show kindness to my child, Onesimus. I became his father in the faith while here in prison. Onesimus hasn't been of much use to you in the past, but now he is very useful to both of us. I am sending him back to you, and with him comes my own heart.

I wanted to keep him here with me while I am in these chains for preaching the Good News, and he would have helped me on your behalf. But I didn't want to do anything without your consent. I wanted you to help because you were willing, not because you were forced. It seems you lost Onesimus for a little while so that you could have him back forever. He is no longer like a slave to you. He is more than a slave, for he is a beloved brother, especially to me. Now he will mean much more to you, both as a man and as a brother in the Lord.

So if you consider me your partner, welcome him as you would welcome me. If he has wronged you in any way or owes you anything, charge it to me. I, PAUL, WRITE THIS WITH MY OWN HAND: I WILL REPAY IT. AND I WON'T MENTION THAT YOU OWE ME YOUR VERY SOUL!

Yes, my brother, please do me this favor for the Lord's sake. Give me this encouragement in Christ.

I am confident as I write this letter that you will do what I ask and even more! One more thing—please prepare a guest room for me, for I am hoping that God will answer your prayers and let me return to you soon.

Epaphras, my fellow prisoner in Christ Jesus, sends you his greetings. So do Mark, Aristarchus, Demas, and Luke, my co-workers.

May the grace of the Lord Jesus Christ be with your spirit. (NLT)

From this letter, we can see the following principles of servanthood:

- **Love**: You can't serve if you don't love. If you say you love others, you must show them you love them. In this example, these two people, though divided by the world, were one in Christ. That love needed to outweigh any issues that divided them in the world.

- **Generosity**: Servants must be generous, because whenever one serves, they give a part of themselves in service.

- **Action:** You can't serve without action. It's wonderful to want to do things, think about doing things, and watch other people do things, but none of these things count as service. Service must be put into action, in the form of doing something relevant and notable for someone else.

- **Kindness:** Service is not wrought in anger, harshness, bitterness, superiority, or any other attitudes that demand other people accommodate someone else. Rather, kindness comes softly, gently, and humbly.

- **Joy:** If you complain while you do it, it won't unite you to your Savior. As people of service, joy should come from sharing the love of Jesus with others.

- **Comfort:** In service, we meet needs. We provide comfort to others by connecting with them. We recognize the need that is met, and we rise to meet it.

- **Faith:** Service is an expression of faith. Anyone can believe in anything (as we see in the myriads of religious experiences present in the world), but not everyone can put their faith into action in the form of service, as those who are in Christ can.

- **Communication:** The Apostle Paul encourages Philemon and Onesimus to a place of mutual service, but he requires they reconcile their relationship, as they are in Christ. That could not be accomplished without communication. Each person needed to convey their needs in the relationship and how they could best serve one another.

- **Responsibility:** Paul was willing to accept responsibility, however it was required. Even though this was not a situation that was his fault or caused by his doing, he stepped up and did what needed to be done. If it means it costs money, if it means it costs time, if it means it costs investment – responsibility speaks loudly in the vision and work of servanthood.

- **Preparation:** The Apostle Paul lastly asked that those reading the letter prepare a guest room for him, so he could visit. In service, we are always prepared for things that may arise, so we can meet any needs.

Looking at examples of servanthood

Philemon and Onesimus are but two examples of servanthood in the Bible. In fact, there are many examples of servants in the Bible we often overlook. Sometimes the ways they served were not always obvious, but they still reveal to us of diversity in service. In the next several chapters, we will look at examples of men who served in different ways in Scripture – and how we can better emulate them in our own living service.

Reflections

- What is your concept of "being somebody?"

- What does "service" mean to you?

- How can you be of service in a deeper way?

- What are some principles of servanthood?

4

THE BELOVED IN THE SONG OF SONGS: A MAN WHO SERVED THROUGH LOVE

————————×( )×————————

PUT [SET] ME LIKE A SEAL [LEAVING AN IMPRESSION ON CLAY, SHOWING OWNERSHIP]
ON YOUR HEART [INSIDE],
LIKE A SEAL ON YOUR ARM [OUTSIDE].
LOVE IS AS STRONG AS DEATH;
JEALOUSY [OR PASSION] IS AS STRONG [TENACIOUS] AS THE GRAVE.
LOVE BURSTS INTO FLAMES [ITS FLAME IS AN INTENSE FIRE]
AND BURNS LIKE A HOT FIRE [OR A GODLIKE FLAME].
EVEN MUCH WATER CANNOT PUT OUT THE FLAME OF LOVE;
FLOODS CANNOT DROWN [FLOOD] LOVE.
IF A MAN OFFERED EVERYTHING [ALL THE WEALTH] IN HIS HOUSE FOR LOVE,
PEOPLE WOULD TOTALLY REJECT IT [OR HE WOULD BE COMPLETELY DESPISED].
(SONG OF SOLOMON 8:6-7, EXB)

- **Reading assignment:** The Song of Songs (Solomon)

The world doesn't tend to regard poets, musicians, thinkers, authors, and yes, even lovers, as "manly men." If anything, the world tends to regard them as the complete opposite. We're told that what defines a man is aggression, anger, force, and disregard for others. That means men who are sensitive, quiet, romantic, musical, or poetic are often considered to be to be outside the boundaries of sexual and gender "norms." (And even if they are, so what?) These men endure teasing, taunting, bullying, and putdowns, often even as adults, from other men in their lives. Even some women look upon such men with suspicion, because they assume something is wrong with them.

It's obvious that men who express emotions or feelings make many uncomfortable, because it seems strange or foreign to them. We treat men who express loving or tender emotions as if they are defective. The truth is that men do have emotions, and they do express them, they just might not manifest in a constructive or altruistic way. Either way, criticizing men who express loving emotion gives men a negative view of love, affection, and interaction with women in a language and demeanor that both can understand. If we are called to be in Christ, then we are called to love each other. We must have expressions of that love and ways to explain and describe it – across the gender spectrum.

The man in the Song of Songs (sometimes known as the Song of Solomon) knew how to serve the special woman in his life. He knew how to express his feelings for her and make her realize she was the most important woman in the world to him. By doing this, the man in the Song of Songs reveals important principles about serving others (especially those closest to us) in our lives. The fact that he is a man, overflowing with affection, desiring intimacy, love and tender emotion makes him even more interesting and relevant, especially as we see through his eyes that the best way to serve anyone is through love.

Emotional and relational servants

There are many ways we can serve others in our lives. The man in the Song of Songs' role as a servant was primarily in an emotional and relational sense, although I am sure the regard he had for this woman and his friends extended into other areas of their lives, as well. From the book, we can see the way he affirmed through words, ideas, concepts, attentiveness, and thoughts, and how they were of great benefit to the woman in his life (and his friends, by extension).

Song of Songs 7:6-9:

How beautiful you are and how pleasing,
my love, with your delights!
Your stature is like that of the palm,
and your breasts like clusters of fruit.
I said, "I will climb the palm tree;
I will take hold of its fruit."
May your breasts be like clusters of grapes on the vine,
the fragrance of your breath like apples,
and your mouth like the best wine.

Sometimes we make service sound like a project instead of a way of life. Yes, service is something we do, but in a bigger way, it is something we are. The man in the Song of Songs recognized this concept. He knew he loved this woman and he needed to show her that love in their everyday lives. If we grab on to the revelation that the most basic principle of service is relationship with others, we've already won half the battle of understanding service and how to serve in our everyday lives.

<u>Men and emotions</u>

We talked a bit earlier about the way society often attempts to make men uncomfortable with feelings. The truth is that it's not all feelings that men are encouraged to avoid, but sensitive gentle, positive, or loving ones, almost exclusively. It starts very young, too. If a boy falls and cries, he is told to "be a man" and stop crying, because "crying is for girls." Have we ever stopped and considered what kind of a message this gives to young boys? They are told that being a man means never being sensitive or in touch with hurt or upset. They're also told being a girl is a bad thing, because girls are in touch with their hurt and upset (i.e., they cry). By telling boys that being emotional is bad, we also tell them that women are bad, because within our culture, we associate emotions and sensitivities with women.

As a result, men learn other ways to outlet their

emotions. The ways that many outlet their feelings are not healthy, in the least. It's not that they don't have them anymore, they simply learn how to outlet them in aggressive or more culturally acceptable ways.

For example, I once knew two male ministers in the area where I used to live. They were notorious for competing with one another. One was using a church building for services because he was dating the granddaughter of the property owner, and they were letting him in under the guise of being "family." The other minister wanted use of the building and felt he had more of a right to it than this other minister, because he was a cousin to the owner, and he didn't have a building of his own. Instead of just working out his feelings, coming to an agreement with the current renter, or going and finding another property, he went to the landlord and told a story about the minister who was renting the building to defame and destroy his character. Then the first minister, feeling attacked, sought to defame the other minister with the exact same accusation in retaliation. Neither of them wound up in the building because the landlord got tired of the drama and threw both of them out.

This is an example of how many men process their feelings. It's not that they weren't emotional or in touch with their feelings (quite the contrary, actually). Instead of doing something constructive with them or feeling them out, one sought to undercut the other and get back at them, due to jealousy. They turned their emotions into ambition and used how they felt to destroy someone else so each could aspire to have a desired or coveted position.

It's obvious that men aren't void of feelings. They are taught to deal with them in a different way. Some of the ways they are taught are both destructive and unchristian. As a result, many men carry this kind of destructive behavior along with them right into the faith, their spiritual lives, and even their relationships.

Enter the man in the Song of Songs. Some say he was Solomon himself; others say the song was written for Solomon. Either way, it doesn't matter. The man in the Song of Songs was so deeply in love with the woman he knew, he didn't care about being macho, or about people thinking he was less than manly, because he had to express how he felt. Rather than feeling aggressive and angry, he was tender and prepared to show this woman just how he felt, at every opportunity.

Song of Songs 4:9-15:

You have stolen my heart, my sister, my bride;
  you have stolen my heart
with one glance of your eyes,
  with one jewel of your necklace.
How delightful is your love, my sister, my bride!
  How much more pleasing is your love than wine,
and the fragrance of your perfume
  more than any spice!
Your lips drop sweetness as the honeycomb, my bride;
  milk and honey are under your tongue.
The fragrance of your garments
  is like the fragrance of Lebanon.
You are a garden locked up, my sister, my bride;
  you are a spring enclosed, a sealed fountain.
Your plants are an orchard of pomegranates
  with choice fruits,
  with henna and nard,
  nard and saffron,
  calamus and cinnamon,
  with every kind of incense tree,
  with myrrh and aloes
  and all the finest spices.
You are a garden fountain,
  a well of flowing water
  streaming down from Lebanon.

We often hear about theories as to why men and women don't understand each other. Some say it is biological, some say environmental, but the man in the Song of Songs disproves the theory that it is impossible for men and women to communicate with each other. If anything, it shows us that men and women can be on the exact same page if they willingly submit to one another and serve each other as humble partners in a relationship.

<u>Enjoying relationships</u>

Expensive weddings. In-laws. Nagging. Bigger apartments. Higher bills. Credit card debt. Date nights. Work schedules. Having to let someone know where you are going. We tend to think of relationships in terms of what they cost us, and we often assume what will cost is high and inconvenient. We hear endless relationship jokes and tease others about being "stuck" in a relationship, especially if someone is male. We don't make relationships sound good for men, and we often downplay monogamy.

I think the reason we don't like relationships is because they drive home the need to serve. Every person, no matter why they enter a relationship, figures out that a relationship requires service, rather than being served all the time. Most people in this world don't seek to be single forever, and that teaches us something about the powerful training ground we have in relationships. Through them, we're called to develop the principles and characteristics God desires each of us to have.

Song of Songs 1:15:

How beautiful you are, my darling!
Oh, how beautiful!
Your eyes are doves.

Song of Songs 2:3-7:

Like an apple tree among the trees of the forest
is my beloved among the young men.
I delight to sit in his shade,
and his fruit is sweet to my taste.
Let him lead me to the banquet hall,
and let his banner over me be love.
Strengthen me with raisins,
refresh me with apples,

for I am faint with love.
His left arm is under my head,
  and his right arm embraces me.
Daughters of Jerusalem, I charge you
  by the gazelles and by the does of the field:
Do not arouse or awaken love
  until it so desires.

Song of Songs 4:16:

Awake, north wind,
  and come, south wind!
Blow on my garden,
  that its fragrance may spread everywhere.
Let my beloved come into his garden
  and taste its choice fruits.

When I first started studying the Song of Songs a few years back, I thought the way the man and woman talked to each other was over the top. I mean, really, nobody talks like that to each other. I could almost picture the two of them falling all over each other, like something out of a sappy musical, as all the birds and flowers suddenly join in song behind them. Even to me, their interaction was a bit of an eye roll, something extremely over the top. (What can I say, my aromanticism was showing!) Now, a few years later, having read, studied, and written on the Song of Songs (my book, *Discovering Intimacy: A Journey Through the Song of Solomon* is available) many times over, I see the interaction between the man and woman in the Song of Songs a little differently.

Sure, most of us probably won't ever break into an eight-chapter long recitation of love over a relationship. I think if any of us even tried to take up such a task, words would probably fail us at some point. Maybe we should think about why that is. I don't think it's because we don't love others, but maybe, just maybe, the world has made us so uncomfortable with relationships that we have trouble articulating how we feel about those in our lives.

The man in the Song of Songs was in touch with how he felt, He knew, he just knew, that they were words he had to express. It wasn't about a one-night stand or a sexual conquest, but a true and abiding love. This woman drove him to be someone better than he was the day before. He knew how important she was to him, and what a treasure he found.

To this man, being in a relationship was about more than just settling down or reaching a certain age where marriage became inevitable. It wasn't about force, everyone else's opinion, or what anyone else told him to do. It didn't happen because of an arrangement. Yes, he found her physically attractive, but that doesn't mean anyone else saw her in quite the same way that he did. But how he found her was more than just physical. He loved this woman, and he saw something special in her. Because of that love, one of the best ways he served – and that all men can serve in their relationships – is by making the person you are involved with know how important they are you, and how valuable they are as a person.

As one striving to be a servant, the first question you need to ask is, do you really know what love is, and are you in touch with it? If you want to serve, and you want to truly be able to touch others and make a difference in their lives, you must first love them. You have to see something within them that is special and transforming and seek to affirm that within them. If you want to be a good servant, that means you need to love: love the whole of people, embrace them and their uniqueness, and show that to them, right where they are.

If you want to find this love balance, enjoy the close relationships you have with others. It is true to say we first learn about servanthood in our intimate relationships. If we have issues serving therein, we are going to have a hard time serving strangers. Being in a relationship with someone else, especially someone you love and care about, should be something you enjoy. Relationships should be approached with excitement and enthusiasm, and should be things that we embrace, rather than dread, in our lives.

I don't mean to suggest that everything about a relationship will be all fun and roses, because service isn't all fun and games. There are points in every relationship that require personal discipline. You won't always feel like loving your partner, nor will you always want to express that love...and you will have the challenge of figuring out how to handle these days, accordingly. Overall, however, being in a relationship should be something that brings you to a greater sense of yourself. In seeing the best in someone else, it gives you the edge to enjoy what you do more and approach the issues that arise with confidence.

Relationships for men

If one is going to serve, one must know – and understand – how to interact in relationships. Most of the time, when we say that someone is "in a relationship" or "not in a relationship," we are referring to someone being in a romantic relationship or otherwise marital relationship, as are the main characters in the Song of Songs. The truth about relationships is far more complicated than dating or marriage. Unless someone lives on an island somewhere with no human contact (think Kevin Costner in *Waterworld*), every one of us has relationships with other people. They aren't all romantic or marital in nature and all are different from the others in some way, but we are constantly in situations that require us to interact with others. Examples include:

- Immediate family (parents, siblings, children)
- Extended family (grandparents, aunts, uncles, cousins, etc.)
- Neighbors
- Acquaintances
- Friends
- Dating
- Engaged
- Married
- Employer/Employee

- Coworker
- Church family

Obviously, these relationships are all different, with different elements to them. What is appropriate with immediate family may not be such with coworkers, and what might work for acquaintances is probably not sufficient with someone to whom you are married. There are all sorts of things that make each one of these relationships different, but there are also many things that bind them together. Above all, all the relationships we have require one common element: every single one of them requires service. If you are going to be in a relationship with anyone, you must be willing to serve, as service is what gives a relationship its edge.

Relationships are often considered "women's territory." Somehow, some way, somewhere, we have given men the idea that they are relationship inept, and unable to connect with others in that specific way. Many are often uncomfortable with relationships, because we give the impression they are all about feelings and interpersonal "female" things. But the truth is that men are involved in relationships, and they can be just fine with them, with the right interest and involvement. This requires having a servant's heart, being prepared to give of self, and being prepared to give, knowing that one won't always get back exactly what they give. Most men understand this at work, with their friends, they might stumble on it with personal relationships, but most do try, and this all means that whether men think so, relationships are anything but "women's territory." They are things that men are a part of, and that if a man is open to so doing, can do very well.

Song of Songs 1:4:

Take me away with you—let us hurry!
  Let the king bring me into his chambers.
We rejoice and delight in you;
  we will praise your love more than wine.
How right they are to adore you!

Song of Songs 3:6-11:

Who is this coming up from the wilderness
*   like a column of smoke,*
perfumed with myrrh and incense
*   made from all the spices of the merchant?*
Look! It is Solomon's carriage,
*   escorted by sixty warriors,*
*   the noblest of Israel,*
all of them wearing the sword,
*   all experienced in battle,*
each with his sword at his side,
*   prepared for the terrors of the night.*
King Solomon made for himself the carriage;
*   he made it of wood from Lebanon.*
Its posts he made of silver,
*   its base of gold.*
Its seat was upholstered with purple,
*   its interior inlaid with love.*
Daughters of Jerusalem, come out,
*   and look, you daughters of Zion.*
Look! on King Solomon wearing a crown,
*   the crown with which his mother crowned him*
on the day of his wedding,
*   the day his heart rejoiced.*

Song of Songs 6:1:

Where has your beloved gone,
*   most beautiful of women?*
Which way did your beloved turn,
*   that we may look for him with you?*

The man and woman aren't the only two people mentioned in the Song of Songs. While they are lovers and their "ultimate song" centers around them, there are also a chorus of friends that follow them around. The couple had other relationships with different people and knew the principle of service with their friends. Their friends loved them, they loved their friends, and they joined in a great song that celebrated not just the couple, but the relationship that all of them had together. The result, as we can see in the Song of Songs, is that service takes us far beyond our personal relationships. The love and service the couple had for one another extended far outside of their own relationship. They knew how to display care and interest in others, and this love echoed back into their own interaction.

Relationships can be complicated, but service in relationships does not have to be. The best approach to relationship service can be summed up by Jesus Christ Himself in Luke 6:31:

Do to others as you would have them do to you.

If you want to be a great servant, then you do for other people what you would want them to do for you. This means being considerate of:

- Their identities
- Their personage
- Their feelings
- Their thoughts
- Their opinions
- Their circumstances
- Their sensitivities

These basic building blocks to serving other people are basic thoughts that revolve around relationships. If one is willing to listen and be attentive to the things going on in someone else's life, it is amazing what one can discover. Relationships don't work without giving a part of ourselves. We give of ourselves as we invest time learning, embracing, and celebrating that other person. In every relationship we're in, we should look for way to more effectively serve and know others.

Taking an interest in others

When I started my study on the Song of Songs, I took a great interest in the woman in the book. She was startling to me, because she was so forward in her desires. Earlier in my life, I was told it was shameful for a woman to be so forward, especially when it came to desire or interest in a physical relationship. When I noticed how forward this woman was, it changed my own perceptions of those stereotypes. It was great for me to see a woman that looked human and was interested in a mate without secret or subtlety. I do believe she is an important role model for women in this regard. What it means to be a woman is not isolated to some Puritanical concept, and the woman in the Song of Songs proves this.

Even though the woman in the book caught my eye, the man and his interaction with her are just as important as hers with him. This was a man who was interested in someone and was not ashamed to stand up and be counted when it came to her. He let his feelings be known, his deep expressiveness toward her, which overflowed into his beautiful, powerful words.

Song of Songs 6:4-10:

You are as beautiful as Tirzah, my darling,
  as lovely as Jerusalem,
  as majestic as troops with banners.
Turn your eyes from me;
  they overwhelm me.
Your hair is like a flock of goats
  descending from Gilead.
Your teeth are like a flock of sheep
  coming up from the washing.
Each has its twin,
  not one of them is missing.
Your temples behind your veil
  are like the halves of a pomegranate.
Sixty queens there may be,

and eighty concubines,
and virgins beyond number;
but my dove, my perfect one, is unique,
the only daughter of her mother,
the favorite of the one who bore her.
The young women saw her and called her blessed;
the queens and concubines praised her.

Who is this that appears like the dawn,
fair as the moon, bright as the sun,
majestic as the stars in procession?

The careful detail, praised through his attention to her, reflects unselfish love and care. He knew her ins and her outs, what was hard for her and what she enjoyed, and wanted to give the best to her, because he was genuinely interested in her. He listened to her prattle on about her night out with the girls, her attempts to match towels for the bathroom, how she felt fat in her jeans, and who she thought gave her the evil eye at the banquet they attended together. He had to listen to her long enough to find out who she was. The more he learned, the more he loved and took a deeper interest in her.

By listening to the woman in his life, this man served her in a powerful way. It helped her feel validated and affirmed and helped her own self-confidence. It gave her a better sense of herself and the reassurance to know someone else cared about her. It might have taken what is perceived as to be a lot of effort on the part of the man, but he gave her exactly what she needed, when she needed it.

Too often we assume that men have a right to ignore others when they are speaking, especially when it comes to relationships or other "menial" aspects of life they find uninteresting. The behavior is justified with everything from biology (which has no basis in fact) to societal ideals that men are not good at relationships or interacting with others. This is also untrue, because we have all seen how intent men can be when they are interested in something. If they think it will increase their chances at work, if it revolves around a hobby or an interest (such as sports or cars) or it is believed to be of profit, it is amazing to note how careful, attentive, interested, and involved a man can be…because he wants to be.

On the 90s show *Home Improvement*, the main character Tim Taylor talks to his neighbor, Wilson, about this very topic. Tim and his wife, Jill, were at odds over his lack of attention to her subtle signals. When he complained of this to his neighbor, Wilson pointed out the various ways Tim might notice his car was malfunctioning. He could tell such by very subtle sounds, smells, and sights, things others might not notice. Through their conversation, Tim realized the problem wasn't that men aren't able to pick up on subtle things. It's an issue of being invested and interested in something and paying attention to the fullest to notice details.

If you are serious about being a servant, you must take an interest in other people, paying attention to what they say, no matter who they are in your life or what you feel about the relevance of the discussion. Why?

James 1:19:

Remember this, my dear brothers and sisters: Everyone should be quick to listen, slow to speak, and should not get angry easily. (GW)

It's not about the subject matter. It's about the person who is talking to you! It's what we used to call respect. No matter how interested in something you might be, your interest in the person should overtake the interest in the subject. If you aren't genuinely interested in others, you can't serve them, because you don't know the best way to reach out and address their needs.

Being an agent of healing

Healing, as we understand it, comes in many forms. While we know there are basic ways to experience healing (and that tends to be the general focus of healing studies) in physical, emotional, mental, or spiritual manifestations, we don't talk nearly enough about the different ways that healing comes about in a person's life or comes through someone else into their lives. As a result, I don't think we properly understand the way we can help someone to heal and the ways that we can also reinforce someone's hurt.

True servants of God seek to help people heal, not hurt. Let's look at some of what the Word tells us about healing.

Proverbs 12:18:

Careless words stab like a sword, but the words of wise people bring healing. (GW)

1 Corinthians 12:28:

In the church God has appointed first apostles, next prophets, third teachers, then those who perform miracles, then those who have the gift of healing, then those who help others, those who are managers, and those who can speak in a number of languages. (GW)

The Bible is clear that healing is what's classified as a charismatic gift. This means it's among the gifts of the church that anyone can receive, at the direction of the Spirit. When we think of healing, we automatically think the gift will manifest by laying hands on sick people and they jump out of wheelchairs or abandon crutches. There's no question this can happen, but the truth about healing is that it is often not that elaborate, nor that dramatic. What is also true is that all of us, as believers with the Spirit within us, can start a healing process, help one, or encourage someone along the way, whether we have a dramatic, showy gift of healing, or not.

Even though we might not be someone with a specific gift of healing, every one of us can be an agent of healing. An agent of healing is someone who believes it is possible to heal and does everything they can to help that process in another. It is often done without a word, a counseling session, a talk, and without either party knowing exactly what healing or what issue they help with within the other individual. We could describe it as caring about another person and being kind enough to someone to recognize that they, as a unique human being, need love, time, attention, and affirmation, and making oneself willing to fulfil that role, as a vessel of spiritual purpose in that person's life.

Song of Songs 1:5-7:

Dark am I, yet lovely,
daughters of Jerusalem,
dark like the tents of Kedar,
like the tent curtains of Solomon.
Do not stare at me because I am dark,
because I am darkened by the sun.
My mother's sons were angry with me
and made me take care of the vineyards;
my own vineyard I had to neglect.
Tell me, you whom I love,
where you graze your flock
and where you rest your sheep at midday.
Why should I be like a veiled woman
beside the flocks of your friends?

The woman in this passage speaks of being "dark, but lovely." This is an ancient reference to being forced into hard labor (because of the disdain her stepbrothers had for her). Being light-skinned was associated with prestige and wealth, because it meant one's skin hadn't been darkened (tanned or burned) by the sun. For this woman to speak of being "dark, but lovely" referred to a deep hurt in her life, something that, every time she looked in the mirror, reminded her of the way she had been mistreated by those of her own house (who were supposed to care about her).

Despite her hurts, she was able to proclaim herself "lovely," which is a powerful accomplishment. She had healed enough in her life to see herself beautiful, despite this glaring issue she saw as a permanent flaw.

It is still obvious, however, that she was still hurting on some level in her life. No matter how far she had come, she still saw herself as "dark." No matter how much her lover told her that she was beautiful, she still saw the "dark" in her life. But there is no question that his constant, emphatic love for her helped the "lovely" part of her to shine through stronger than the "dark" that reminded her of her difficult and painful past.

Every one of us comes into relationships with things that leave us "dark, but lovely." These are the things that we learn to live with, our life hurts that dwell under the surface and bubble up periodically. They are reminders of what others did to us, how we felt at the time, what we lived through, and it doesn't typically take much to bring them right up again, vivid and alive with the thoughts and feelings associated with them.

Being a servant and being an agent of healing (even if it's not specifically a gift you have) means recognizing these things and not making the deliberate overture to reemphasize insecurities and hurts in someone's life. When you get to know someone well enough to know what will hurt them and what won't, a true servant doesn't inflict that pain upon them. Servants of God need to watch their words, attitudes, the things that they say in passing that appear to be a joke (but are not), the coarse jesting or jokes they make at other people's expense or that might be designed to give an underhanded message, the negative remarks and attitudes we convey to express dislike or disapproval, the way we carry ourselves in our body language, and the way we will express things non-verbally through facial expressions. We are constantly giving people impressions of our thoughts, attitudes, beliefs, and ideas, and in servanthood, we need to make sure we aren't giving people the wrong idea about our feelings towards them.

Encountering issues in service

Let's not assume the man and woman in the Song of Songs had no problems. The Bible always reflects real life and real-life issues, so I don't believe the Song of Songs was ever intended to be taken as some sort of fairy tale featuring

Cinderella and Prince Charming. It wasn't a Hallmark movie. I'm sure there were times when the couple fought and argued over diapers and whose turn it was to take out the trash. Some nights she wanted Italian, and he wanted Chinese. Work schedules impeded date nights. There were days when they didn't see eye-to-eye, and he probably didn't understand her very well (and vice versa). They probably blew up at each other every now and then, having those good old-fashioned arguments that classic television glorified. They had periods where they didn't talk as she slept on the seam of the mattress, or he slept on the couch. Great passion, like the two in the Song of Songs displayed, leads to very intense relationships. That means when the fight is on, they mean it as much as the time when they decide to make up. Even though they had periods where they were mad at each other, it didn't change the love that the two of them had. The thing it probably did effect, in a complicated way, was the way they served one another.

Song of Songs 3:1-5:

All night long on my bed
I looked for the one my heart loves;
I looked for him but did not find him.
I will get up now and go about the city,
through its streets and squares;
I will search for the one my heart loves.
So I looked for him but did not find him.
The watchmen found me
as they made their rounds in the city.
"Have you seen the one my heart loves?"
Scarcely had I passed them
when I found the one my heart loves.
I held him and would not let him go
till I had brought him to my mother's house,
to the room of the one who conceived me.
Daughters of Jerusalem, I charge you
by the gazelles and by the does of the field:
Do not arouse or awaken love
until it so desires.

It's important to remember that being a servant is not something most people feel like doing consistently. Our feelings and thoughts about situations change. We have times where we don't like what is required of us. Service is something that still takes an effort, and is something that we need to walk out, no matter what's going on that day.

The tough news with this realization is that if we are going to be serious servants, we are going to do it, as the Bible talks, "in season and out of season." Our level of service cannot be based on what anyone else is doing, thinking, or even how you are feeling at that time. Whether you are mad at someone or not, whether it's convenient or not, you still must do what God has called you to do and do it in a way that is in accord with Christian principle.

Not everyone receives the service that we offer to them. There are times when it's time to pack it in and move forward, shaking the dust off our feet as we go. Many of us have spent years trying to serve people that are not our assignment, nor are they people who receive what we have. Sometimes we need to just pull ourselves together, lick our wounds, and move forward to our own healing as we find joy in serving others, rather than in spending time on people who do not want to receive the service we give.

I am not going to dwell on this much. It is something we encounter, but I am not going to give much attention to it. After a while, we tend to use our own hurt as an excuse to stop serving. We want to find a reason not to make the effort and we capitalize on people's response to what we do as an excuse not to do it anymore. Whether we serve the people we are around for a lifetime or serve them for a little while, we are still called to make connections with people and help them along, walking with them in relationship and interacting as servants. This doesn't change because we get hurt in the process. As people connected to the body that's supposed to serve one another, this is where the service of others is designed to step in – bless us – and have their support to help us keep going.

Serving in love and intimacy

The man in the Song of Songs shows us, firsthand, that being involved with other people costs us something. In that cost, we find something even greater. Service wrought in love abides by this same principle. It costs us something, but in it, we get something back that is even deeper or more purposed.

Song of Songs 7:1-5:

How beautiful your sandaled feet,
O prince's daughter!
Your graceful legs are like jewels,
the work of an artist's hands.
Your navel is a rounded goblet
that never lacks blended wine.
Your waist is a mound of wheat
encircled by lilies.
Your breasts are like two fawns,
like twin fawns of a gazelle.
Your neck is like an ivory tower.
Your eyes are the pools of Heshbon
by the gate of Bath Rabbim.
Your nose is like the tower of Lebanon
looking toward Damascus.
Your head crowns you like Mount Carmel.
Your hair is like royal tapestry;
the king is held captive by its tresses.

If we are going to serve others in love and especially serve those who are closest to us, we must be considerate. If we know people, love them, learn their ups and downs, and their wounds and feelings, it brings us to a place where consideration becomes a natural part of our lives. We know what might offend, but we don't seize the opportunity. We know what someone likes, so we make the effort to do that. We avoid being trite or mean, and in love, working to help and serve them helps us to work out the different difficulties, pitfalls, and shortcomings that we ourselves have as people.

It works both ways and produces a great result.

Does the man in the Song of Songs sound inconsiderate? Does it sound like a man who demanded certain rites, privileges, or roles out of his wife? Does he sound like a man who, when his wife was sick, expected her to behave as normal or take on certain roles to cater to him? The answer to this is a resounding no! Even though she might have been sick and difficult, maybe didn't receive what he did with ease, or even put up a fight at times, he still saw through that and saw her deeper needs, her deeper need for healing, and he persisted to love and serve, even when she didn't make it easy for him to do so. He loved her that much, and that love moved him to serve.

In summary, the man in the Song of Songs shows us that intimacy and love are possible for men. Relationships are not foreign to them. If a man can master love, he can master service. It will manifest itself in many ways, but all those ways relate to his character and the way he will interact with other people, especially those closest to him. Even though we don't consider love and relationships to be catalysts for service, they are. In fact, love and relationships are the two foundations we will find in every situation related to service. We can learn much about service just by being, doing, and embracing consideration, love, and appreciation for others. If we make that effort, our service follows in kind.

Reflections

- Do relationships make you uncomfortable? Why or why not?

- Do you have a hard time expressing emotion? What are some ways you can work on this?

- How can you take more of an interest in those who are around you?

- What's a primary way you express love for others?

How do others know you love them?

- When it comes to being an agent of healing, how do you help in this process with others? How can you help it in a greater way?

5

THE PHILOSOPHER OF ECCLESIASTES: A MAN WHO SERVED THROUGH WISDOM

————————x( )x————————

DO NOT PAY ATTENTION TO EVERY WORD PEOPLE SAY,
OR YOU MAY HEAR YOUR SERVANT CURSING YOU.
(ECCLESIASTES 7:21)

- **Reading assignment:** The Book of Ecclesiastes

E cclesiastes isn't a commonly studied book of the Bible. I'd venture to say it's a book that most people do not understand well, because of its author's perspective. Many Christians disregard philosophers and thinkers in general, thus we aren't making room for the truth that is the book of Ecclesiastes. The man who sat back, looked over his entire life, and declared much of it to be vanity doesn't sound like a man that many in today's church would engage with very well. In pursuit of all the things he did, said, lived, and experienced, the philosopher of Ecclesiastes had to step back, survey it, and discover that there wasn't much point in having it all if God wasn't in any of it.

The truth is that we need more dialogue, thought, and insight in our church and our world today, just like we find in Ecclesiastes. We need people to step back, look at things, think about them, the consequences, and the results. From this, we must piece together the different parts of human existence that make us exactly who we are. Thought, discussion, and ideas are an integral part of what makes the Bible the Bible and what makes Christianity, Christianity. Both are based on long-standing oral traditions, written words, thoughts, discussions, debates, and ideals to result in the thoughts and feelings we have about our faith today.

Here we are going to pay tribute to another way to be of service in the Kingdom: through wisdom and knowledge. Even though every man reading this book may not have the status of a philosopher, everyone has something to offer, some way they can use wisdom and knowledge to serve someone else in this life.

Servants of wisdom and knowledge

We don't tend to associate service with wisdom and knowledge. Why? We often associate wisdom and knowledge with a certain level of vanity. We think people who know things always have to have the last word and are showy about their knowledge. It's not wrong to believe there are people like this out there, who use the information they have to show off before the whole world. This is true with any field of subject: there is always someone who feels the need to distort an entire area of study to make sure the focus is on them. This doesn't nullify the field or area of interest, however. There are many people who recognize education and endowment of information as important aspects of life. There will forever be people who, in contrast to those who make it all about them, seek to offer others something valuable in deposit of knowledge.

Ecclesiastes 1:12-18:

I, the Teacher, was king over Israel in Jerusalem. I applied my mind to study and to explore by wisdom all that is done under the heavens. What a heavy burden God has laid on mankind! I have seen all the things that are done under the sun; all of them are meaningless, a chasing after the wind.

What is crooked cannot be straightened;
  what is lacking cannot be counted.

*I said to myself, "Look, I have increased in wisdom more
than anyone who has ruled over Jerusalem before me; I
have experienced much of wisdom and knowledge." Then I
applied myself to the understanding of wisdom, and also of
madness and folly, but I learned that this, too, is a chasing
after the wind.*

For with much wisdom comes much sorrow;
  the more knowledge, the more grief.

Thus enters the book of Ecclesiastes, and the man known to us as the "philosopher" or "teacher." As a former philosophy major, his demeanor and writing style reflect that of a true philosopher. Thinking – and perhaps, in some instances, overthinking – was natural to him. He thought he had all the answers until he got out there and lived, and then he discovered nothing at all. That made him step back and think even more. He was sincere and serious, almost to the point of being grave, as he tried to discover the meaning of life. He knew life was to be lived, so he took every opportunity he had to do everything, and go everywhere, experience it all. At the end of it, he didn't quite find what he expected. His search for meaning and purpose changed his life. As he thought more, studied more, looked to more, and discovered more, he documented his experience and encounters of wisdom and knowledge.

The words we have in this book are a result of his process. He shared his wisdom and knowledge with us, not to rub in our faces that he did, thought, and lived large, but because there is important information and empowerment in his words. By writing Ecclesiastes, the philosopher of the book served us through his wisdom. He gave us a piece of himself and his life. Iin that service, we are better for it if we take what he has said and apply it to our own lives.

Wisdom and knowledge in trusted counsel

We hear a lot about the need for mentors and advisors because society has finally discovered what the Bible knew all along: there is something good in having trusted guidance and counsel in one's life. When people have mentors and advisors in their corner, they do better at work, in their personal lives, and they feel better in their confidences and self-esteem as individuals. Being able to talk things out with someone trusted, see things from a different angle, get practical advice, and navigate through everything from ordinary to difficult situations makes life that much easier and that much more encouraging.

Proverbs 15:22:

Without counsel purposes are disappointed; but in the multitude of counsellors they are established. (KJV)

These benefits come from the wisdom and knowledge present in trusted counsel. When we offer counsel, we deposit wisdom into someone else's life. This is a form of serving others. This type of service is one of the most important forms of service, even though we don't often think of it in that way. It is important because:

- **It teaches us to honor different gifts and abilities:** The Bible makes it very clear we don't all have the same gifts and abilities. What God gives to one, He doesn't always give to someone else. The reason for this? We are all one body. Just as we are one body with many different parts that serve different functions, so too the church has many different gifts present to meet all needs present. Acknowledging wisdom and knowledge as service helps us embrace mentors and advisors who help us launch into successful places and to be more comfortable with our own abilities. They help us recognize that what we have to offer is just as valuable as what they have to offer.

- **It helps edify others:** We might talk a good game about edification, but I don't think we understand the first thing about it. We encourage people to fall into pits or traps, and then we stand back and point fingers, causing them to stumble. This is not the true definition of Biblical edification, which means we build others up. If we rightly understand edification, we should be building people up in what is true and right rather than puffing them up in anything that comes along. True edification leads to a better and more spiritual place than leading people into any old, completely wrong place.

- **It shares life experience that helps others to avoid mistakes:** All of us have made mistakes in our lives, both big ones and small ones. Somewhere along the way, we hopefully learned from those mistakes so we can make better choices and decisions (that work) in our lives. Mentors and advisors take the practical experiences they had and give people the wisdom and knowledge they have learned from their experiences. This helps others can see the consequences in actions and avoid making those mistakes in their own lives.

- **It makes us aware that we don't have to make mistakes generation after generation, and that living life doesn't have to mean making so many mistakes:** We often assume that making mistakes, especially the ones our ancestors made, is a given. Service involving wisdom and knowledge teaches us the opposite. Even though our ancestors might have made mistakes, that doesn't mean we have to make them ourselves, all over again. Yes, we do make mistakes in life, but it doesn't mean that we must make the same mistakes that other people made, or that we must make so many mistakes ourselves. Life is not contingent on making multiple mistakes and walking into various traps. We can avoid the issues that others have faced if we make better choices. It is through mentorship and advisors that we find ourselves empowered to do this.

- **It makes people of any age feel purposeful:** I don't believe mentors have to all be over a certain age in order to advise others, just that they need to be proficient in whatever area they serve as mentor. This gives all people of all ages purpose, direction, interest, and enthusiasm about what they do and where they are going. It gives our lives meaning.

- **It inspires education:** Education is often downplayed as being irrelevant or unnecessary. There are many different forms of education. With those different forms of education come different types of knowledge that help us to be well-rounded, balanced people. Having good mentorship in our lives encourages us to seek more, learn more, and delve into topics in a deeper way, and transform our view of the world and ourselves.

- **It gives perspective to knowledge and wisdom:** Wisdom and knowledge can sound intimidating and far off, like something for some strange, distant person who is way smarter than everyone else. We think that thinking is just for people with high IQs who like to sit around and think all day. Wisdom and knowledge aren't just for the super-smart. They are important, practical and applicable things for our everyday lives, and every one of us can walk in wisdom and knowledge, whether we are super-smart, or not.

<u>Older men mentoring younger men</u>

In New Testament times, the Apostle Paul advised the following in Titus 2:1-2, 6-10:

You, however, must teach what is appropriate to sound doctrine. Teach the older men to be temperate, worthy of respect, self-controlled, and sound in faith, in love and in endurance... Similarly, encourage the young men to be self-controlled. In everything set them an example by doing what is good. In your teaching show integrity, seriousness and soundness of speech that cannot be condemned, so that those who oppose you may be ashamed because they have nothing bad to say about us.

Teach slaves to be subject to their masters in everything, to try to please them, not to talk back to them, and not to steal from them, but to show that they can be fully trusted, so that in every way they will make the teaching about God our Savior attractive.

When I was a new believer, I breezed past passages like these because I thought I knew more than everyone else. I was saved less than a year and I thought I had more Bible insight and identity into Christian living than anyone else did. The sad part was that with some people I knew, I was right; I did know more than they did. That just fueled the idea that nobody could possibly have anything to tell me about Christian living that I needed to hear.

Now when I hear this kind of attitude in younger believers, it grieves me. In my day, that kind of attitude was seen as a situation that called for discipline. Someone would attempt to sit a person like this down and educate them, showing them that there were many things they needed to be prepared for in their spiritual lives. Even though it was generally understood that most new believers should be in the "New Believer's Class," someone usually took a new believer under their wings and made sure that they had the time and attention they needed to come into spiritual maturity.

Some of what the Apostle Paul mentions here might seem redundant. Why would we need to be reminded that older men should set a good example for younger men, and that younger men need to be taught to be self-controlled, doing good, and serious about what they do? Most of us would probably think this is a given, but I can testify by watching the state of the church that many don't think twice about allowing younger believers and church members, at that, to behave any way they like. We don't tend to require an example of older members, and younger members don't have serious examples and mentors in the faith to bring about true conversion and discipleship.

God knew we needed structure in the church. Beyond the church, we need structure as people. We need people to help us out, and we need to be people who help, as well. We need the balance of wisdom service and those we serve, seeing that those who serve aren't just giving aimless advice, but are living it in their own lives, in a visible way.

Ecclesiastes 3:9-15:

What do workers gain from their toil? I have seen the burden God has laid on the human race. He has made everything beautiful in its time. He has also set eternity in the human heart; yet no one can fathom what God has done from beginning to end. I know that there is nothing better for people than to be happy and to do good while they live. That each of them may eat and drink, and find satisfaction in all their toil—this is the gift of God. I know that everything God does will endure forever; nothing can be added to it and nothing taken from it. God does it so that people will fear him.

Whatever is has already been,
and what will be has been before;
and God will call the past to account.

Mentors who operate in service can't be living however they please. The whole purpose of having a mentor is to model the way they live and the things they do to achieve success. The old saying, "Do as I say, not as I do" cannot apply in the life of a true servant who mentors through wisdom. Those who mentor are called to live as examples with their lives as much as they do with their words. Mentors are to be overcoming role models, those who, although certainly not perfect, know how to fight against the tides of conformity and error and come to a lasting place of triumph.

<u>Balancing life</u>

Most people have a hard time with the balances necessary to maintain the different aspects of life they pursue. It's almost a universal statement to say that work dominates most of the people's time, followed by household responsibilities and family time, leisure time, church and spiritual time, and other activities that individuals consider to be important. Add to that mix attempting to balance other schedules (spouse, children, parents, friends, events) while figuring out one's own. With so many things going on, most people's lives reflect serious imbalances based on need and guilt. It's not uncommon to see people dealing with serious levels of stress, anger, frustration, and intolerance for the things around them. Life lived in stress leads to regret, regret leads to upset, and upset leads to states of sadness and depression, where people feel like their lives have no value or purpose.

Ecclesiastes 3:1-8:

There is a time for everything,
and a season for every activity under the heavens:

a time to be born and a time to die,
a time to plant and a time to uproot,
a time to kill and a time to heal,
a time to tear down and a time to build,
a time to weep and a time to laugh,
a time to mourn and a time to dance,
a time to scatter stones and a time to gather them,
a time to embrace and a time to refrain from
embracing,
a time to search and a time to give up,
a time to keep and a time to throw away,
a time to tear and a time to mend,

a time to be silent and a time to speak,
a time to love and a time to hate,
a time for war and a time for peace.

The Bible is clear there is a time for everything in our lives. This list isn't a "to-do" checklist, but the realization that our lives revolve around various seasons, opportunities, and balances as we confront work, tasks, responsibilities, worship, rest, and leisure. We can't get away from this fact. A true servant moving in wisdom won't let people off the hook with their excuses of being too busy. The old adage, "If it's important to you, you'll make time" is very true, and also very revealing as to what is most important to us. Sometimes we need to reduce the number of activities, sometimes we need to readjust our priorities, and at other times we need to declutter our lives, but no matter how you put it, a true and wise servant will bring us back to the principle of a time for everything and a season for all things.

One of the major things most lives lack comes from wisdom servants: those who help us to see what is most important and how to gain better insight into the things that are true priorities. Most people today are so busy and so preoccupied with so many things, they don't have the spiritual reflection or needed "down time" to gain perspective of life and the balance of what is really important.

As Jesus and his disciples were on their way, He came to a village where a woman named Martha opened her home to Him. She had a sister called Mary, who sat at the Lord's feet listening to what He said. But Martha was distracted by all the preparations that had to be made. She came to Him and asked, "Lord, don't You care that my sister has left me to do the work by myself? Tell her to help me!"

"Martha, Martha," the Lord answered, "you are worried and upset about many things, but few things are needed—or indeed only one. Mary has chosen what is better, and it will not be taken away from her." (Luke 10:38-42)

We've all heard the story of Martha and Mary: two sisters who appear to represent two opposites. I think there's a bit of Martha and Mary in all of us...and far more Martha than we are apt to admit. We take comfort in being so busy, in meeting expectations, and in showing off in front of others (especially if we want to impress someone). Martha didn't want Jesus to think she was a bad hostess. She judged Mary for sitting still and listening to Jesus, and then exploded when He didn't reprimand Mary for her conduct.

Overworked, over-extended people expect others to adopt the same behavior. They look down on those who rest or pause for a few moments as lazy. The truth is not that everyone else is lazy (and if they are, that's a different issue). It's that the overworked aren't setting the necessary boundaries in their lives to find appropriate balance.

Life changes. It's not reasonable to think we can do all the same things we always did, at least at once. Wisdom calls us to pay attention to times and seasons, how things do change, and that we need to be aware and purposed for the duration in our lives. Our good mentors and wise servants help us to discern times and seasons, to know what should dominate our focus and our time, and recognize what is needed right here and now, in this season.

Service present in giving counsel and advice

In one sentence, giving counsel and advice is all in how it is done. You can either give advice to better someone's life, or you can give advice to be the center of attention. Either way, the choice is yours. Giving advice to change someone's life can do just that, so giving advice must be approached with wisdom and caution and purposed through the true heart of a servant.

Ecclesiastes 7:1-13:

A good name is better than fine perfume,
  and the day of death better than the day of birth.
It is better to go to a house of mourning
  than to go to a house of feasting,

for death is the destiny of everyone;
  the living should take this to heart.
Frustration is better than laughter,
  because a sad face is good for the heart.
The heart of the wise is in the house of mourning,
  but the heart of fools is in the house of pleasure.
It is better to heed the rebuke of a wise person
  than to listen to the song of fools.
Like the crackling of thorns under the pot,
  so is the laughter of fools.
  This too is meaningless.

Extortion turns a wise person into a fool,
  and a bribe corrupts the heart.

The end of a matter is better than its beginning,
  and patience is better than pride.
Do not be quickly provoked in your spirit,
  for anger resides in the lap of fools.

Do not say, "Why were the old days better than these?"
  For it is not wise to ask such questions.

Wisdom, like an inheritance, is a good thing
  and benefits those who see the sun.
Wisdom is a shelter
  as money is a shelter,
but the advantage of knowledge is this:
  Wisdom preserves those who have it.

Consider what God has done:

Who can straighten
  what He has made crooked?

It is my opinion that giving advice is highly overrated. As a minister, I have given a lot of advice in my day. People come, claiming to be sincere and desperate, and hang on to most of what you say. When they leave your office or hang up the phone, the situation quickly becomes different. Most people don't follow the advice given and are quick to fall right back into their original patterns, time after time. For something that everyone wants to dispense, it can be a frustrating and futile project. It can easily aggravate the servant who gives the advice.

It is true that experience is often a cruel and necessary teacher for many. There are those who don't listen to sound counsel, no matter who gives it, or for any reason. Yet even in the dark recesses of frustration over wasted advice, there are those who do follow advice. Even though it might not happen most times or in many cases, there are times when people get desperate enough to follow sound advice. That means that, as a wisdom servant, being able to give a sound word of counsel or advice is an important thing. It is something that can help someone find a better path, changing their direction from its current course.

Men tend to get awkward when it comes time to receive or accept advice. Society tells men it's a sign of weakness to need help, and that includes needing advice or guidance from someone else. This means it is especially important for a man to give advice to another man (or to anyone, for that matter) from a servant's heart, done in love, rather than as a dictator, mocking a man for his mistakes. The message that men don't need guidance is a dangerous one. All human beings need a word and guidance from time to time. If men think they don't need assistance, or when they do reach out receive an offensive attitude, they won't reach out for it and continue to make mistakes. It also means they will never learn how to appreciate wisdom, and they won't accept it from the women in their lives (when it comes through them), either. Being able to receive advice is a humbling process for anyone, and this means that when advice is given, it needs to be done with the right heart and approach.

Giving wise counsel and advice are not just a practical service; they are also a spiritual gift. It takes divine insight, wisdom, and perspective to give someone a word of advice that is both practical and applicable. Contrary to popular belief, it is not something everyone can do. Even though many might think they have something valuable to offer a situation, having the servant's heart of wisdom and the gift to deliver it is truly irreplaceable, especially in our world today.

In the New Testament, we learn about the charismatic gifts that are open to all believers. We will talk more about these gifts in a later chapter, but two of these gifts are known as the word of wisdom or the word of knowledge. Both gifts are based on the giving of advice from a divine perspective. The word, advice, and knowledge given comes from God through the individual that gives it, rather than the human person giving advice based on their own information or experience. Even God knows a word in due season is important, and He chooses to send it through servants who are endowed with His gifts from on high!

Beware chasing after vanity

One of the main themes of Ecclesiastes is the uselessness of life when it is approached without wisdom. The philosopher is trying to teach us about the danger of chasing vanity. Wisdom can serve as a powerful combatant in the war against vanity and vain living.

Ecclesiastes 2:1-11:

I said to myself, "Come now, I will test you with pleasure to find out what is good." But that also proved to be meaningless. "Laughter," I said, "is madness. And what does pleasure accomplish?" I tried cheering myself with wine, and embracing folly—my mind still guiding me with wisdom. I wanted to see what was good for people to do under the heavens during the few days of their lives.

I undertook great projects: I built houses for myself and planted vineyards. I made gardens and parks and planted all kinds of fruit trees in them. I made reservoirs to water groves of flourishing trees. I bought male and female slaves and had other slaves who were born in my house. I also

*owned more herds and flocks than anyone in Jerusalem
before me. I amassed silver and gold for myself, and the
treasure of kings and provinces. I acquired male and
female singers, and a harem as well—the delights of a
man's heart. I became greater by far than anyone in
Jerusalem before me. In all this my wisdom stayed with me.*

*I denied myself nothing my eyes desired;
  I refused my heart no pleasure.
My heart took delight in all my labor,
  and this was the reward for all my toil.
Yet when I surveyed all that my hands had done
  and what I had toiled to achieve,
everything was meaningless, a chasing after the wind;
  nothing was gained under the sun.*

Vanity is a false sense of security and pride in the things that
one can do or accomplish themselves (such as work,
money, appearance, or qualities). In more spiritual terms,
vanities are idols. They are empty in and of themselves, but
we look to them because we have some part in their
fashioning. We would be amazed if we considered how
common vanity is, and how many ways it disguises itself as
joy, satisfaction, or pleasure in accomplishment. It manifests
as we hold fast to everything that is fleeting or vanishing in
this world rather than holding to the spiritual things of God.
Vanity is often lurking right under the surface, avoiding the
deeper questions of life: why does this bring you joy and
what is at the root of it? Can you take corrections? Do you
avoid solid, good advice? Can you accept defeat when it
comes, and consider that God has something else in store
for you?

The church itself has become exceedingly vain over the
past several years. Whether chasing riches, prestige, fame,
political connections, or worldly successes, none of these
things will follow us into the next life. If we break down the
behaviors encouraged within churchgoers, much of it is
vainglorious and vain-seeking. So much emphasis on what
we have or don't have, how things appear, the connections

that people make, the jobs or professions that we have, how much we give to the church, and the partiality that is often expressed in one way or another toward those who are wealthy (only to make them wealthier) all break down to vanity.

Men pay a particularly high price in the pursuit of vanity. They hear they should pursue it both from the world and now from the church. Men are told that everything in life is about their accomplishments: the better job, the bigger house, the fancier car, the good-looking wife. Seldom do we teach men about the kind of character they should have, or about how empty life is when it is spent chasing after every single vain thing that surrounds them. It is possible to have every achievement and every vain thing in this world and still have nothing, as impossible as that might sound. This also means that men have their own unique pitfalls and traps when it comes to vanity that relate to appearance, expectations in relationships, employment, and willingness to participate in family life.

Ecclesiastes 5:8-20:

If you see the poor oppressed in a district, and justice and rights denied, do not be surprised at such things; for one official is eyed by a higher one, and over them both are others higher still. The increase from the land is taken by all; the king himself profits from the fields.

Whoever loves money never has enough;
whoever loves wealth is never satisfied with their income.
This too is meaningless.

As goods increase,
so do those who consume them.
And what benefit are they to the owners
except to feast their eyes on them?

The sleep of a laborer is sweet,
whether they eat little or much,

but as for the rich, their abundance
    permits them no sleep.

I have seen a grievous evil under the sun:

wealth hoarded to the harm of its owners,
    or wealth lost through some misfortune,
so that when they have children
    there is nothing left for them to inherit.
Everyone comes naked from their mother's womb,
    and as everyone comes, so they depart.
They take nothing from their toil
    that they can carry in their hands.

This too is a grievous evil:

As everyone comes, so they depart,
    and what do they gain,
    since they toil for the wind?
All their days they eat in darkness,
    with great frustration, affliction and anger.

This is what I have observed to be good: that it is appropriate for a person to eat, to drink and to find satisfaction in their toilsome labor under the sun during the few days of life God has given them—for this is their lot. Moreover, when God gives someone wealth and possessions, and the ability to enjoy them, to accept their lot and be happy in their toil—this is a gift of God. They seldom reflect on the days of their life, because God keeps them occupied with gladness of heart.

Good counsel helps avoid the pitfalls of vanity and the temptations it offers. The wisdom of good counsel reminds someone that vanity is, indeed, vanity and that chasing vanity will lead to nothing fulfilling in the long run. Instead of looking for the accolades of the world, it is more important to pursue the things of God, pursue meaningful relationships, and foster a true and balanced perspective, experiencing many things in life and loving the pursuit of life itself.

Remembering to seek after what is important

The greatest reminder that any of us can get from wise counsel, whether in detailed, specified, or summary form, is the bottom line of the philosopher's advice in the book of Ecclesiastes. That reminder is that as people, we need to seek what is important. Too often in life we pursue the things we think we are supposed to pursue. As a woman, I have written much about these expectations for women, but I am not blind to the fact that we have them for men, as well. The expectations on men can be just as burdensome, unkind, and difficult to pursue as the ones that those of other genders are pressured to explore. God doesn't ask us to be miserable or chronically lost in our lives. He does ask us to follow those things which will lead us to a sense of importance and fulfillment, and what those things are may very well vary between people.

Ecclesiastes 9:7-10:

Go, eat your food with gladness, and drink your wine with a joyful heart, for God has already approved what you do. Always be clothed in white, and always anoint your head with oil. Enjoy life with your wife, whom you love, all the days of this meaningless life that God has given you under the sun—all your meaningless days. For this is your lot in life and in your toilsome labor under the sun. Whatever your hand finds to do, do it with all your might, for in the realm of the dead, where you are going, there is neither working nor planning nor knowledge nor wisdom.

The most important thing anyone can do if they are called to serve through wisdom is offer it in a way that shows others the important things in their own lives. This means every wisdom servant has a defining moment where they recognize the need to step back, let God intervene, and help someone else to move forward. The promises of life that everyone hopes to discover and achieve are found as we apply God's wisdom and knowledge in ways that are understandable for our own lives. It is thanks to every wisdom and knowledge servant that those moments, those ideals, and yes, even those divine changes are that much more manageable and understandable.

Reflections

- Do you have an easy time receiving counsel from others? Why or why not?

- Do you balance your time well? Are there areas where you can do better?

- What do you think are your greatest achievements in your life?

- How do you define "vanity?"

6
JOB: A MAN WHO SERVED DESPITE BEING A VICTIM

━━━━━━━━━━●( )●━━━━━━━━━━

THEN THE LORD SAID TO SATAN, "HAVE YOU NOTICED [CONSIDERED; SET YOUR HEART ON]
MY SERVANT JOB? NO ONE ELSE ON EARTH IS LIKE HIM. HE IS AN HONEST AND INNOCENT MAN,
HONORING GOD AND STAYING AWAY FROM EVIL [1:1]."
(JOB 1:8, EXB)

- **Reading assignment:** The Book of Job

When you have a men's conference, odds are good the preacher doesn't tell everyone to flip to the book of Job for insight. In fact, I can't recall the last time I heard a preacher tell everyone to flip to the book of Job, period. The way that Job suffered for a period and his difficulties were authorized by God Himself doesn't comfort most modern churchgoers. In an atmosphere where we constantly hear that God wants us to prosper and God only gives us good things, Job's experience doesn't make sense.

No matter how much Job might not make sense to modern churchgoers, he is still in the Bible, along with his difficult and trying ordeal. It speaks to us about life, experiences, suffering, victimization, and learning to find meaning in the things that are hard or uncomfortable for us. Job also shows us the importance of being a servant and holding fast, no matter how difficult things may be at that point in time, especially when there is no end in sight.

Job makes us uncomfortable. Job makes us look at ourselves in a deeper way, to see if we are believers when more is required of us than makes us comfortable. If all the vanities and things of life we hold dear vanish tomorrow, can we still be faithful? Will we still serve, and do it well? If we hurt, will we still serve? If it's just you and God, will you still be able to do what He asks of you to do? These are all questions that a true servant must answer to determine the level of service that shall bring forth fruition in someone's life.

When being blameless doesn't reap a reward

Several years ago, we were in a spot where the rent was due on our church property, and we didn't have a way to pay for it. Things had been going reasonably well with my business and with our ministry work, right up until Christmas came. Even though none of our church members were preoccupied with the holiday, we were surrounded by other people who were – and that meant their lack of giving to the ministry or desire for business services caused us to come up financially short. We had money saved up that turned out to be enough for about a month and a half, but when the money was gone, it was gone...and it wasn't easily replaced. At the same time, a large bill came due, and a member of our church was short on money for their own household rent. The inevitable conversation came up: why was this happening, and why was it happening now? We had all been faithful, doing what we knew God was directing us to do, so why were we being left without the resources to do what needed to be done?

What I wound up pointing out is that sometimes we don't suffer from doing the wrong thing; we suffer for doing the right thing. It doesn't make sense in our natural minds, and it doesn't make sense in the scope of what we are often taught. From the time we are children, we are told that if we do something bad, we will be punished. If we do something good, we will be rewarded. We grow up with this same type of thinking, believing that if bad things happen to us, it's because we are being punished for doing wrong. In the spiritual realm, this is not always the case. Sometimes we do everything right, we aren't doing anything we shouldn't be doing, and that makes us more of a target for the enemy. We go through because we do right. As unfair as it might feel, as wrong as it might be, it is part of being a believer. Even though we did get our rent paid (we figured out a way to close the space in the lean times), there are many, many times in our Christian walk where things happen to us that feel unjust, and we are left to sort out the "Why God?" questions through our unfair situations.

Job 1:1-12:

A man named Job lived in Uz. He was a man of integrity: He was decent, he feared God, and he stayed away from evil. He had seven sons and three daughters. He owned 7,000 sheep and goats, 3,000 camels, 1,000 oxen, 500 donkeys, and a large number of servants. He was the most influential person in the Middle East.

His sons used to go to each other's homes, where they would have parties. (Each brother took his turn having a party.) They would send someone to invite their three sisters to eat and drink with them.

When they finished having their parties, Job would send for them in order to cleanse them from sin. He would get up early in the morning and sacrifice burnt offerings for each of them. Job thought, "My children may have sinned and cursed God in their hearts." Job offered sacrifices for them all the time.

One day when the sons of God came to stand in front of the LORD, Satan the Accuser came along with them.

The LORD asked Satan, "Where have you come from?"

Satan answered the LORD, "From wandering all over the earth."

The LORD asked Satan, "Have you thought about My servant Job? No one in the world is like him! He is a man of integrity: He is decent, he fears God, and he stays away from evil."

Satan answered the LORD, "Haven't you given Job a reason to fear God? Haven't you put a protective fence around him, his home, and everything he has? You have blessed everything he does. His cattle have spread out over the land. But now stretch out your hand, and strike everything he has. I bet he'll curse You to Your face."

The LORD told Satan, "Everything he has is in your power, but you must not lay a hand on him!"

Then Satan left the LORD's presence. (GW)

Job wasn't targeted by Satan because he was a rebellious, difficult person. He was Satan's choice because the Bible says he was blameless. He was doing everything he could to live the right and proper way. In other words, Job became a challenge for Satan. He was going to pull out every stop to get Job away from God, because he was so upright and moral.

That's one of the major reasons people who are doing right seem to go through trying periods. If we break down our lives from an objective perspective, no one goes through all the time, no matter how self-pitying we may feel when we think all we do is "go through." What happens to us is exactly what happened to Job, in a certain sense: we are attacked for a period, the attack that we go through is difficult and intense, and then we come out on the other side.

Even though we all go through, we tend to look down on people who go through things to the point of being victimized or intimately wounded by someone else. This is true of women in our society, who are blamed for rape or for abuse, but it is also especially true for men in a way that we are often uncomfortable discussing. When a man is victimized in any form, we tend to not just blame him, but look down upon him, as if he is less of a man because of what happened to him. He may be hesitant to get help or to talk about it, especially in the alpha male setting present in today's church. We don't like to think anything breaks through the tough, masculine exterior that we have come to associate with manhood. We regard anyone who has any other exterior other than the stereotype as not being "masculine enough."

I've taught for many years that being saved doesn't mean being Superwoman for women. It doesn't mean taking on every single issue, problem, or cause in the world (or even in your own life, for that matter). It's fine, and yes, very Christian, to embrace the principle of healthy boundaries and limits in one's life. The same is true for men. Being saved doesn't mean you turn into Superman and are able to fight all the world's ills, let alone ignore or immediately overcome the problems you might have in your own life. Being a Christian means walking out that life with God, one moment at a time, and encouraging each other through our own limitations as we experience the attacks of the enemy for getting through.

There is something to be said just for surviving. It may not often feel like it, especially when a victim is left to put the pieces of their lives back together and live in the same skin they were in, as everyone now looks at them differently. In Job, we see the power of overcoming and the importance in serving victims as well as seeing the way that overcomers of trauma can serve all of us.

Men who are victims

We are fooling ourselves if we think we have never been victimized, regardless of gender. Every person in the world is a victim of someone else's sin. It might not be in ways that are extremely noticeable or harmful in the long term, but all of us have experienced the injustice that sin inevitably brings into our lives. We've all had points in time where we have been treated badly, without mercy, mistreated, abused, and left for someone else to try to repair or help alone. Yes, some ways are more damaging than others, but the reality is that none of us are free from victimization. There are things that hurt us (whether we admit to it or not) and there are things that damage the image we have of ourselves, sometimes in a way that requires more than an attempt to shake whatever it is away from our souls.

Victimization among men is an unspoken reality, one that many men experience behind the scenes as they go about their everyday lives. It's not something they asked for, that they deserved (nobody deserves to be a victim) or that was a "stripe" to earn to make it in the world. It's something that hurt, something that caused and inflicted pain, and it was something that, whether we like to admit it or not, was unfair. The unfairness of it does not dissipate because it happened to a man, nor is it right to have the attitude that a man should just be able to shake it off and act like it never happened. A man who goes through has the right to admit what happened to him and to state that whatever it was, was unfair, unjust, and wrong.

Ignoring the truth that men are often victims of abuse, sexual misconduct, societal indoctrination, confusing messages (we train them to be killers in the military and in brutal situations in general and then criticize them for not being sensitive), self-inflicted ignorance, violence, injustice, ill treatment, and disrespect doesn't make any of it go away. It didn't happen because they weren't manly or masculine enough (there are many instances where alpha male behavior escalates circumstances like this), or because they were somehow of diminished capacity to be a man. It happened because they live in a world that often doesn't care about other people and as a result, they got caught in a selfish, evil crossfire.

This all relates to Job in a very simple way: Job was a victim. No matter how much preachers today try to scour the Bible for passages that somehow prove Job deserved what happened to him, he didn't. He wasn't a perpetrator of some deep, hidden sin, and no matter how much anyone might want to answer to the contrary, the whole point of Job was that he wasn't someone who was out to do something wrong. Some things just happen because they do, because we are alive and breathing and encounter the wrong situations at the wrong moments, and the same is true with Job and many victims who are alive to tell their stories today.

Job 30:20-31:

"I call to You for help,
  but You don't answer me.
    I stand up, but You just look at me.
You have begun to treat me cruelly.
  With Your mighty hand You assault me.
You pick me up and let the wind carry me away.
You toss me around with a storm.
I know You will lead me to death,
  to the dwelling place appointed for all living beings.

  "But God doesn't stretch out His hand against one who is ruined
    when that person calls for help in His disaster.
Didn't I cry for the person whose days were difficult?
Didn't my soul grieve for the poor?
When I waited for good, evil came.
When I looked for light, darkness came.
My insides are churning and won't calm down.
Days of misery are ahead of me.
I walk in the dark without the sun.
I stand up in public and call for help.
I'm a brother to jackals
  and a companion of ostriches.
My skin turns dark and peels.
My body burns with fever.
So my lyre is used for mourning
  and my flute for loud weeping. (GW)*

Job reminds us that we need to not only serve men who are victims but also allow them to serve as a part of their healing process. Those who are suffering need a kind word, empathetic support, and our love and our trust, not encouragement to ignore what has happened or, worse yet, violate them in a different way with attitudes that reflect lack of interest or caring. What Job needed more than anything throughout his experience was the ability to process what he was going through, express himself, ask his questions, and gain insight into the deeper meanings of life through his own suffering and discomfort. The breakthrough he received in the end wasn't just about the turnaround of his material life, but about the spiritual insight that he gained by overcoming his difficult and victimizing situation. He was able to handle all he received because he received God's greater grace to get through it, and triumph despite it and over it.

The praying servant

I cannot ever underestimate the relevance of prayer in a servant's life. If there's one thing we should note about Job, it is that he must have had an incredible prayer life. There are people who gripe about Job, forgetting he had an ongoing dialogue with God throughout his trial, when they can't even pray for five minutes.

We often don't take prayer as seriously as we should in church. Saying we will pray for someone is overused, and often not ever done. We speak of "thoughts and prayers" as if it nullifies the Christian responsibility to mourn with those who mourn. We callously tell someone else we will pray for them, then not only do we not do it, but we also don't check in or seek to help someone else with whatever it is that they are going through. Then we have the extreme of those who use prayer as a gossip forum (and men do it as much as women do), to get the dirt on someone else's life and the next thing you know, they are on the phone with someone else under the guise of "prayer," spreading the story around. The result is a general lack of respect and regard for prayer, as people find offers for prayer veiled in distrust, disregard, and lack of genuine concern or care for what is going on in their life.

It makes me recall a recent situation where I spent far

longer than I should have considering whether to buy a dress online. The online store doesn't take returns. That, however, wasn't the real issue behind my feelings. The dress was made by a seller who specialized in "modest clothing," meaning the attire met specific standards of "holiness wear." I didn't know how I felt endorsing such. When I spoke with the designer, she explained that she custom makes the clothing to our specifications and was willing to do alterations for free if necessary. I decided to take the plunge, sent my measurements, and placed the order. Shortly after, I received a message from her telling me that order was an answered prayer, as she was praying for another order that month.

I could have sat back and overlooked the situation further under the guise of prayer, or I could have done what I did and stepped up to be the answer to her prayer. Prayer should not be used as an excuse to refrain from serving in some other way that might be an answer to someone's existing prayers. It should also not be of no value or purpose, especially if you are in a situation where you can't do anything yourself. Prayer is a form of service, not exclusively, but in part, combined with true devotion and encouragement that can be offered to others. True prayer shows that someone cares, they are interested in the things that interest others, and that they recognize help comes in many forms, the font of our help coming from God. This means that prayer is something that is vital for our spiritual – and natural – lives, and offering prayer is an important part of service.

Job 10:1-22:

"I hate my life.
I will freely express my complaint.
I will speak as bitterly as I feel.
I will say to God,
'Don't condemn me.
Let me know why You are quarreling with me.
What do You gain by mistreating me,
by rejecting the work of Your hands

while You favor the plans of the wicked?
Do you actually have human eyes?
Do you see as a mortal sees?
Are your days like a mortal's days?
Are your years like a human's years?
Is that why You look for guilt in me
and search for sin in me?
You know I'm not guilty,
but there is no one to rescue me from Your hands.

"'Your hands formed me and made every part of me,
then You turned to destroy me.
Please remember that You made me out of clay
and that You will return me to the dust again.
Didn't You pour me out like milk
and curdle me like cheese?
Didn't You dress me in skin and flesh
and weave me together with bones and tendons?
You gave me life and mercy.
Your watchfulness has preserved my spirit.
But in Your heart You hid these things.
I know this is what You did.

"'If I sin, You watch me
and will not free me from my guilt.
How terrible it will be for me if I'm guilty!
Even if I'm righteous, I dare not lift up my head.
I am filled with disgrace
while I look on my misery.
Like a proud, ferocious lion you hunt me down.
You keep working Your miracles against me.
You keep finding new witnesses against me.
You keep increasing Your anger toward me.
You keep bringing new armies against me.

"'Why did You take me out of the womb?
I wish I had breathed my last breath
before anyone had laid eyes on me.

Then it would be as if I had never existed,
as if I had been carried from the womb to the tomb.

'Isn't my life short enough?
So stop this, and leave me alone.
Let me smile a little
before I go away
to a land of darkness and gloom,
to a dismal land of long shadows and confusion
where light is as bright as darkness.
I'll never return.'" (GW)

Most of the time when we think of prayer, we think of women in prayer around the altar or the old church mothers praying us through our difficult times. At other points, we think of our deliverance moments, those points of contact where prayer brought about visible change. Many times, I have found that men come to me for prayer because they assume prayer to be a "woman's thing." They assume that they can't go to a man with their prayer requests. I have even heard stories where a man went for prayer and was accused of not being a man for his prayer request. This kind of logic is absurd, because I do hope – and pray (pardon the expression) – that we can overcome it with some better understanding of just what prayer is and how much of a service it is to the church.

Prayer isn't a gendered activity. It's communication. Yes, there are many types of prayer that celebrate many different things (including thanks, intercession, praise, and petition), but overall, prayer doesn't have to be or seem so complicated. Prayer is our communication with God. We pray when we take the time to communicate with God, either silently (speaking to Him internally) or verbally (out loud). We can pray in a group or by ourselves, and as hard as it might be to imagine, we can even pray while we are doing something else (such as working or doing a repetitive task). It is how we talk to Him, how we relate to Him, and how we voice our needs and concerns to Him. Even though prayer tends to be something we feel needs to be formal or scheduled, it doesn't have to be. All you need to do to pray is address your Father, state your prayer or your need, say whatever else is on your heart, and then conclude it in Jesus' Name. Let's remember how Jesus taught us to pray:

Pray, therefore, like this: Our Father Who is in heaven, hallowed (kept holy) be Your Name.

Your kingdom come, Your will be done on earth as it is in heaven.

Give us this day our daily bread.

And forgive us our debts, as we also have forgiven (left, remitted, and let go of the debts, and have given up resentment against) our debtors.

And lead (bring) us not into temptation, but deliver us from the evil one. For Yours is the kingdom and the power and the glory forever. Amen. (Matthew 6:9-13, AMPC)

You can pray right where you are. It doesn't have to be filled with fancy words or the eloquence often heard in the pulpit. As long as it is sincere and heartfelt, your prayer is received in reverence.
  Job 14:1-22:

"A person who is born of a woman is short-lived and is full of trouble.
He comes up like a flower; then he withers.
He is like a fleeting shadow; he doesn't stay long.
You observe this
and call me to account to You.

"If only an unclean person could become clean!
It's not possible.
If the number of his days
and the number of his months are determined by You,
and You set his limit,

then he cannot go past it.
Look away from him, and he will cease to be.
Meanwhile, he loves life as a laborer loves work.
There is hope for a tree when it is cut down.
It will sprout again.
Its shoots will not stop sprouting.
If its roots grow old in the ground
and its stump dies in the soil,
merely a scent of water will make it sprout
and grow branches like a plant.
But a human dies and is powerless.
A person breathes his last breath, and where is he?
As water drains out of a lake,
or as a river dries up completely,
so each person lies down
and does not rise until the heavens cease to exist.
He does not wake up.
He is not awakened from his sleep.
I wish You would hide me in Sheol
and keep me hidden there until Your anger cools.
Set a specific time for me when You will remember me.

"If a person dies, will he go on living?
I will wait for my relief to come
as long as my hard labor continues.
You will call, and I will answer You.
You will long for the person Your hands have made.
Though now You count my steps,
You will not keep a record of my sins.
My disobedience will be closed up in a bag,
and You will cover over my sins.
As surely as a mountain falls
and rocks are dislodged,
so water wears away stone,
floods wash away soil from the land,
and you destroy a mortal's hope.
You overpower him forever, and he passes away.
You change his appearance and send him away.

His sons are honored, and he doesn't know it.
Or they become unimportant, and he doesn't realize it.
He feels only his body's pain.
He is only worried about himself." (GW)

In looking at Job's prayer life (which was quite intense) we also learn we can pray for ourselves and it be empowering and effective, instead of waiting for someone else to come along and do it for us. Sometimes we need to be of service to ourselves and get in there and pray. Job's long experiences – and interludes – with prayer show us prayer as a service not just for other people, but to gain insight and depth within ourselves. Sometimes the experience we have with prayer isn't to bring about a big, huge change in life that manifests through things, but to bring about a radical change in the individual themselves. Through prayer, we not only speak, but also listen, and God reveals things to us that change our lives and our ideas about life as we regularly communicate with Him.

Men, if you want to grow spiritually and gain power with God, then you need to have a solid prayer life. It doesn't make you weak to talk to God. In talking to God, you will find the strength and wisdom needed to move forward in life and to gain better insight into the spiritual gifts you have so you can better use them. It's also powerful to pray for those in your life, whether it's your spouse, kids, boss, friends, parents, church community, or those you cover. It helps you to be a better man, it gives you a wonderful avenue for service for others, and it also helps to prepare you for greater service. The more you look around you and see situations and circumstances through the eyes of prayer, the better equipped you will be to reach out in the right way, at just the right time.

It's not the answer that's the problem, it's the question

How many times have people come to you, irate and looking for advice, only to find themselves angry because they didn't like the advice you gave them? If you are in leadership, a parent, maybe even in a relationship at some point in time, you have probably had this experience. Better yet, you have also probably been on the other end of the experience, where it was you seeking advice and then got angry when the advice wasn't what you wanted it to be.

Have you ever thought back over these experiences and looked at them through a different lens? If you have, you probably laughed in hindsight over your reaction or, better yet, how you responded to the situation. Odds are good that you looked at your question, your position, and your feelings quite differently, because you were no longer in that situation anymore.

In many instances in Job, the dialogue he and God have is most interesting. Job will ask a question (or in some instances, a series of them), and then God would answer Job. Sometimes God answered Job, sometimes He didn't. The purpose of this ancient method of discussion was to make Job look at himself, look at his question, and look at the very basis of his argument again, to come to a different conclusion.

Job 38:1-38:

Then the LORD answered Job out of the storm.
Who is this that belittles My advice
with words that do not show any knowledge about it?
Brace yourself like a man!
I will ask you, and you will teach Me.

"Where were you when I laid the foundation of the earth?
Tell Me if you have such insight.
Who determined its dimensions?
Certainly, you know!
Who stretched a measuring line over it?
On what were its footings sunk?
Who laid its cornerstone
when the morning stars sang together
and all the sons of God shouted for joy?

"Who shut the sea behind gates
when it burst through and came out of the womb,
when I clothed it with clouds
and wrapped it up in dark clouds,
when I set a limit for it
and put up bars and gates,
when I said, 'You may come this far but no farther.
Here your proud waves will stop'?

"Have you ever given orders to the morning
or assigned a place for the dawn
so that it could grab the earth by its edges
and shake wicked people out of it?
The earth changes like clay stamped by a seal,
and parts of it stand out like folds in clothing.
Wicked people are deprived of their light,
and an arm raised in victory is broken.
Have you gone to the springs in the sea
or walked through the valleys of the ocean depths?
Have the gateways to death been revealed to you,
or have you seen the gateways to total darkness?
Have you even considered how wide the earth is?
Tell Me, if you know all of this!

"What is the way to the place where light lives?
Where is the home of darkness
so that you may lead it to its territory,
so that you may know the path to its home?
You must know because you were born then
and have lived such a long time!
Have you been to the warehouses where snow is stored
or seen the warehouses for hail
that I have stored up for the time of trouble,
for the day of battle and war?
Which is the way to the place where light is scattered
and the east wind is spread across the earth?

"Who made a channel for the flooding rains
and a path for the thunderstorms

to bring rain on a land where no one lives,
on a desert where there are no humans,
to saturate the desolate wasteland
in order to make it sprout with grass?
Does the rain have a father?
Who gave birth to the dewdrops?
From whose womb came the ice,
and who has given birth to the frost in the air?
The water hardens like a stone,
and the surface of the ocean freezes over.

"Can you connect the chains of the constellation Pleiades
or untie the ropes of Orion?
Can you bring out the constellations at the right time
or guide Ursa Major with its cubs?
Do you know the laws of the sky
or make them rule the earth?
Can you call to the clouds
and have a flood of water cover you?
Can you send lightning flashes so that they may go and say
   to you,
'Here we are'?
Who put wisdom in the heart
or gave understanding to the mind?
Who is wise enough to count the clouds
or pour out the water jars of heaven
when the dirt hardens into clumps
and the soil clings together? (GW)

Job proves to us that it's not the answer that's the problem, it's the question. At some point in our lives, we have all asked questions that sound an awful lot like the ones that Job asked:

- Why is there suffering?
- Where is God when natural disasters happen?
- Why do bad things happen to good people?
- Why me, God?

The questions are a part of natural inquisitiveness and pique the curiosity of human thought. The reality is, however, that the problem isn't the answer. We are seeking an answer to something that has, in some way or another, already been answered within our human existence. Instead of going over and over these questions, we need to examine ourselves and what we are doing when such situations come up, and how we can be of better service in the world around us.

One of the most powerful ways that we serve other people is by making them examine themselves. Whether it is in the form of good advice, in the form of questions that make others think, or in the form of encouragement and deep wisdom, we are helping other people to grow and look at life from an eternal perspective.

Service through friendship

Have you ever stopped to wonder why shows such as *Friends* were such big hits? Sure, there is something to be said for having a great idea at the right time and striking the right chord with a generation of viewers at the precise moment in history. But why is it that a show like *Friends* ever struck a chord with audiences to begin with? The reason is simple: people embraced the friendship of the characters, spanning a decade, and the way they unconditionally loved and supported one another. The reason *Friends* was a huge hit is because it demonstrated a level of friendship that replaced the immediate family of childhood and made it seem possible that those characters could be real friends, or any of our friends, during the duration of the show's history. *Friends*, and shows like it, reminded (and continue to remind) all of us that friends are important.

Job's friends weren't the best in the world. Even though they did sit with him for a week as he mourned, they didn't seem to come up with anything constructive to say. They certainly weren't people I would want to get stuck with on a deserted island. Job was down and out, he didn't do anything to deserve what was happening to him, and instead of helping him, they found ways to make him feel like he was the problem. We look at them and we can't imagine how Job ever considered them friends, why he considered them friends, or that he spent time listening to and entertaining them as friends while he was going through one of the most difficult situations of his life.

Job 6:14-30:

"A friend should treat a troubled person kindly,
even if he abandons the fear of the Almighty.
My brothers have been as deceptive as seasonal rivers,
like the seasonal riverbeds that flood.
They are dark with ice.
They are hidden by snow.
They vanish during a scorching summer.
In the heat their riverbeds dry up.
They change their course.
They go into a wasteland and disappear.
Caravans from Tema look for them.
Travelers from Sheba search for them.
They are ashamed because they relied on the streams.
Arriving there, they are disappointed.

"So you are as unreliable to me as they are.
You see something terrifying, and you are afraid.
Did I ever say, 'Give me a gift,'
or 'Offer me a bribe from your wealth,'
or 'Rescue me from an enemy,'
or 'Ransom me from a tyrant'?
Teach me, and I'll be silent.
Show me where I've been wrong.
How painful an honest discussion can be!
In correcting me, you correct yourselves!
Do you think my words need correction?
Do you think they're what a desperate person says to
* the wind?*
Would you also throw dice for an orphan?
Would you buy and sell your friend?

"But now, if you're willing, look at me.
I won't lie to your face.
Please change your mind.
Don't permit any injustice.
Change your mind because I am still right about this!
Is there injustice on my tongue,
or is my mouth unable to tell the difference between right
   and wrong? (GW)

We've all been stuck with Job's friends, though. Every one of us has gone through something where those closest to us just didn't understand. Instead of just admitting that and offering comfort, they did and said things to make us feel worse. We were at our lowest point, having the worst time we could imagine, and we were left feeling even worse as our friends didn't take the time to stand with or behind us. They tried to figure out what we did, why we did it, what we did wrong, and at the end of it all, we just wanted to drive a big stake through our ear canal to drown out the noise of our unhelpful "friends."

Worse yet...we've all been Job's friends. I know, I know, a major "ouch" moment. Truth be told, we have all had situations where we dropped the ball and didn't support our friends like we should have. We sat in judgment, looked down on them, made them feel small or isolated, or made comments to the effect that somehow blamed them for what they were going through. Instead of being servants, we sat high and looked low, playing the role of unhelpful and judgmental critics toward those that we are supposed to love and support.

Being a friend isn't easy. We think it's easy because we love our friends and like to be around them as a rule. When it comes to friendship, though, the reality of being a friend is that it isn't something all that easy to do when it counts. It certainly isn't that easy to do on a regular basis. Being a true friend means offering a part of yourself to your friends and, in the process, laying down a part of yourself.

John 15:13:

Greater love has no one than this: to lay down one's life for one's friends.

Up and dying for our friends probably won't accomplish much for them in the course of our ordinary lives. While this verse was certainly true in Jesus' case and in the case of those who physically sacrifice their lives for their friends, there are other ways we can understand it and that we should think about when it comes to friendship. Whenever we do something for someone else: whether it's listening to them, being there for them, supporting them, caring about them, or just doing things with them, we give part of ourselves to them. The way that we lay down our lives for our friends in an everyday context is by being servants. As we make ourselves available to our friends, we serve them.

John 15:15:

I no longer call you servants, because a servant does not know his master's business. Instead, I have called you friends, for everything that I learned from My Father I have made known to you.

Many years ago, when I was a much younger Christian than I am now, I went to interview the pastor of a church in the area about his religious beliefs for a college project. He belonged to a denomination with a colorful past and a sordid reputation among the Christian community, but he was an interesting young pastor who had some very radical (at least radical for 20 years ago within his denomination) ideas about faith, the Christian life, and evangelization. When I asked him about activities for evangelism, such as going door-to-door, he said to me, "We need to get out there and be people's friends." All these years later, what he said to me then still sticks with me. It's vitally important that we, as Christians, know how to be friendly and how to maintain friendships, and how to serve one another as friends.

There have been many Christian books written on the importance and virtue of friendships between women. It seems obvious and logical to Christian writers to write about Christian women and their relationships, because women tend to be more overt about their love and care for their true friends when they find them. It is also more common for Christian women to develop friendships almost exclusively with other Christian women, thus excluding a lot of opportunity for witnessing through friendship (and making their relationships a curiosity for study). There have not been many books about the friendships of Christian men, or how important friendship is in the lives of men. For men to develop positive friendships within the Christian faith is just as important as it is for women. While I do not recommend that anyone exclusively have Christian friends, men need to have Christian friends just like women have Christian friends. They need the support, encouragement, and commonalities that women need, and the concept that as they go along in this journey, they are not alone.

If you are going to make the commitment to serve through friendship, that starts with making yourself a better friend. While many men want to do it, many still are unsure of where to start. Here are some ideas for becoming better friends:

- Pray for your friends and with them.
- Don't be afraid to talk to your friends or to listen to them.
- Do things with your friends, such as watching a game or go out to eat somewhere that you all like.
- Spend time together without the wives and kids.
- Start a Bible study among your friends.
- Call and check up on your friends to see how they are doing.

When you have the wrong friends at your service

Job's friends make us aware of the powerful way that friendship serves as a form of service to others. The question becomes, what do we do when we have a bunch of friends who are just like the ones Job had? If you are the one who is always making all the overtures, the one who always makes all the calls, or the only one who seems concerned with anyone else, it is likely there is a problem somewhere in the relationship connect. If you go through difficult things or they go through them and either one of you can't seem to be there to support the other, then there is a problem.

If you are finding yourself in Job's position or finding yourself to feel more like Job's friends in a situation, it is probably time to look at that. Let me make it clear that we need to be cautious on how we assess ourselves in these different situations. You may very well be going through a bad time because of something that you did, and that does make your situation different from Job's, especially if you refuse to admit what you have done that's wrong. Our problems do not exclusively consist of the devil and haters. Yes, you might need support and certainly forgiveness, but neither one comes to people who refuse to face themselves and admit their flaws. It's easy to blame a hard situation on lack of support when the reality is that you don't have the support you might like because of what you did or how you are acting.

Once upon a time, I covered a woman who had an uppity, self-righteous attitude. She thought very highly of herself. Instead of treating me as her leader, she treated me as if I was a distant acquaintance, a source of competition. After a while, it got both trying and frustrating to deal with her. Soon she dropped off the planet...until an opportunity came for her to publish a book with my company. To make the long story very short, she continually dodged appointments and lied about not receiving paperwork under the guise of having a "hard time" in her life. If you took her at face value, she was having a hard time because she was going through a marital separation, and her husband was withholding money. If you looked her up online, however, you would find mugshots of her during this interim, because she broke the law. She wasn't going through for righteousness, but because she got caught breaking the law and had to answer for that.

I would have been much more tolerant if she had been upfront and honest about her circumstances. The fact that she both withheld information and lied to me about what was going on made it so I didn't particularly care about her "hard time" and wanted nothing further to do with her. Sometimes we drain people (or they drain us) with constant and incessant craziness, drama that is caused by either connecting to the wrong people or doing the wrong things ourselves. Thus, we need to assess the following when we consider the situations that we have with our friends:

- Am I doing anything to cause the problems that I am having?
- Are my associations with others causing me problems?
- Is there anything I can do to change the tide for the circumstances I am in?

It is also possible that you can examine everything, step back in honesty, and conclude that you have outgrown a friendship in your life. Sometimes we outgrow relationships in our lives, and our friendships are no different. If you find yourself unable to be there for your friends or your friends there for you, it might be a sign that you are just at a point where it is time to make new friends and move to a new level in life.

Job 2:11-13:

When Job's three friends heard about all the terrible things that had happened to him, each of them came from his home—Eliphaz of Teman, Bildad of Shuah, Zophar of Naama. They had agreed they would go together to sympathize with Job and comfort him.

When they saw him from a distance, they didn't even recognize him. They cried out loud and wept, and each of them tore his own clothes in grief. They threw dust on their heads. Then they sat down on the ground with him for seven days and seven nights. No one said a word to him because they saw that he was in such great pain. (GW)

Job's friends most likely didn't start out as such problematic acquaintances. At one point in his life, they were there with him all the way, excited and happy about the things going on in his life. They probably shared some great times, fun experiences, prayed for each other, and enjoyed their lives together. After all, the Bible does describe them as "friends," not enemies. If they'd started out as unsupportive, we wouldn't hear about them at all. This tells us something very key about Job's situation. What Job went through took him to a whole different dimension of life, and this is not at all unreasonable to conclude from his experience. Sometimes we go through very difficult and trying experiences and they change us, and it is not always in a negative or embittered sense. Sometimes the things we go through change our outlook on life, give us wisdom and knowledge, change our desires, the things we want from our lives, and the priorities we have. While Job's friends might have been fine to serve him before all this started, they were not prepared nor able to serve him while he went through or after his transformation.

Friends help get you through what you go through. Having the wrong people around makes what you go through worse. It is also hard for people who don't know what to do for you. If you have people like this in your life, it's time to replace them with others. Always refrain from offense when you are replaced during a new season in someone else's life. It just means they aren't equipped to go where you are heading, either.

Service "without stuff"

When people are asked what they know about Job, they always immediately say, "He lost everything he had!" Our first thoughts of Job are what he lost and how he suffered, but seldom do we ever think of Job as "He learned to live without everything he ever had." Why don't we ever think of

Job in this light? Why is the focus always on what he had and didn't have anymore, rather than on what he gained in his state of lack?

We focus on what Job lost because we don't like to lose things. We think we couldn't live – or serve God – without all the comforts and perks we have. We don't like to think God would authorize us to go through a period of lack as a trial or test of our faith. More than just a test of our faith, Job proved that not only could he survive without all the conveniences and comforts of life, he could still love and serve God, even when he didn't understand what was happening to him.

Job 1:13-22:

One day when Job's sons and daughters were eating and drinking wine in their oldest brother's home, a messenger came to Job. He said, "While the oxen were plowing and the donkeys were grazing nearby, men from Sheba attacked. They took the livestock and massacred the servants. I'm the only one who has escaped to tell you."

While he was still speaking, another messenger came and said, "A fire from God fell from heaven and completely burned your flocks and servants. I'm the only one who has escaped to tell you."

While he was still speaking, another messenger came and said, "The Chaldeans formed three companies and made a raid on the camels. They took the camels and massacred the servants. I'm the only one who has escaped to tell you."

While he was still speaking, another messenger came and said, "Your sons and your daughters were eating and drinking wine at their oldest brother's home when suddenly a great storm swept across the desert and struck the four corners of the house. It fell on the young people, and they died. I'm the only one who has escaped to tell you."

Job stood up, tore his robe in grief, and shaved his head.

Then he fell to the ground and worshiped. He said,

> *"Naked I came from my mother,*
> *and naked I will return.*
> *The LORD has given,*
> *and the LORD has taken away!*
> *May the name of the LORD be praised."*

Through all this Job did not sin or blame God for doing anything wrong. (GW)

We often forget God desires us, not all the stuff we offer in place of ourselves. Yes, we are required to tithe and give of ourselves financially from the resources we have. These things aren't a substitution for the sacrifice of our lives, however. We like to offer our things in place of ourselves because we think that's easier – it means we must give less – but it is not what God requires of us. It's very possible to give tons and tons of stuff, be a top contributor to the church, donate lots of things to charity, but still not be right with God.

I've known many men who think giving things makes up for time spent with family, friends, even God. They'll give their kids over and above what they need and sometimes even excessively dote on their spouses to compensate for spending too much time at work, away from home, not spending any quality time as a couple, or not spending time with the children. This concept that money or things can replace the person themselves spills over into many men's relationships with God. The idea that just a little more money or a little more giving can substitute for the time and discipline God requires is a temptation that many give into over the years.

This is based on a root of pride that judges people (including self) by material possessions and financial wealth. It's the message that if we have things, we are all right, better than someone else, or more competent at what we do. They are all messages the world gives, especially to men, and reinforces that what makes a man is the ability to be a "provider." Job wasn't any less of a man because he fell on hard times. If anything, he became more of a man because he was still willing to serve, to hold fast, and to keep going even though he was in pain and duress. He wasn't less of a man because he had to rely on someone else (in this case, God) to help him through the circumstances that he didn't invite, nor desire, in his life. Some of the best servants in history walked out their lives of service with very few material things and a lot of help from a community of believers or with the support of those involved. It didn't make any of them less human. It raised their own awareness of what it meant to be a human being and a child of God in a deeper and more profound way.

Job proves to us that we don't need to have a lot of things to serve God, because it's not our things that God (nor the devil) really wants. The devil might very well use things to keep us from God or to try and get us away from God, but he really doesn't care about our stuff in the long run, either. What both God – and the enemy seek – are us. Trying to bribe God with our things, move Him with what we have, or putting things in between Him and us is not going to get us where we need to be with Him.

Job learned that he could serve God just fine without all the things he'd grown accustomed to have. He could be a servant without his family, friends, money, cattle, farm, house, and material wealth. He was able to serve through sickness and blight, emotional distraught, pain, discomfort, and trial. No matter what trial was thrown at him, he kept serving God. When he was encouraged to curse God and turn his back on Him, Job kept serving. He might have missed his family and his past wealth and prosperity, but he knew that without a right relationship with God, the things he had would be meaningless.

The "stuff" we have in this life can easily be lost. History is full of economic losses, financial downturns, cultural collapses and the shifting of nations. Economic power changes hands, wealth leaves families, and bad investments can be generational game changers. Whether we have stuff or not, God still expects us to serve Him and develop a deep relationship with Him, no matter how much we have.

Service through suffering

The last thing that we can see in Job as relates to service (at least that we will be looking at in this book) is the way that Job served through his suffering. Suffering is one of those topics that the modern church doesn't desire to touch with a pole. It's something that got so out of control historically that nobody desires to investigate or understand it in a deeper sense for right now. That means books like Job not only make us uncomfortable, but they also fall through the cracks of essential understanding and study, meaning we don't know what to do when we fall into situations like Job's. If we hear at church that we shouldn't ever have to go through anything, we genuinely will expect that's the way it should be. We find ourselves rebuking the devil anytime we go through. It's easy to look at situations in such a black and white manner, only seeing them from what we lose, rather than looking deeper into suffering and what it is from it that we sometimes should gain.

Job 7:1-21:

"Isn't a mortal's stay on earth difficult
like a hired hand's daily work?
Like a slave, he longs for shade.
Like a hired hand, he eagerly looks for his pay.
Likewise, I have been given months that are of no use,
and I have inherited nights filled with misery.
When I lie down, I ask,
'When will I get up?'
But the evening is long,
and I'm exhausted from tossing about until dawn.
My body is covered with maggots and scabs.
My skin is crusted over with sores; then they ooze.
My days go swifter than a weaver's shuttle.
They are spent without hope.
Remember, my life is only a breath,
and never again will my eyes see anything good.

The eye that watches over me will no longer see me.
Your eye will look for me, but I'll be gone.
As a cloud fades away and disappears,
so a person goes into the grave and doesn't come back
  again.
He doesn't come back home again,
and his household doesn't recognize him anymore.
So I won't keep my mouth shut,
but I will speak from the distress that is in my spirit
and complain about the bitterness in my soul.

"Am I the sea or a sea monster
that you have set a guard over me?
When I say,
'My couch may give me comfort.
My bed may help me bear my pain,'
then You frighten me with dreams
and terrify me with visions.
My throat would rather be choked.
My body would prefer death to these dreams.
I hate my life; I do not want to live forever.
Leave me alone because my days are so brief.
"What is a mortal that You should make so much of him,
that You should be concerned about him?
What is he that You should inspect him every morning
and examine him every moment?
Why don't You stop looking at me
long enough to let me swallow my spit?
If I sin, what can I possibly do to you
since You insist on spying on people?
Why do you make me your target?
I've become a burden even to myself.
Why don't you forgive my disobedience
and take away my sin?
Soon I'll lie down in the dust.
Then You will search for me, but I'll be gone!" (GW)

Buddhists teach that we suffer because we form attachments to things in this world. They believe if human beings stop holding onto things in this life, people can achieve true happiness. When Buddhists meditate on nothingness or try to figure out hard puzzles rather than focus on worldly interests, they try to get one step closer to achieving the state where they eliminate suffering. It's an interesting theory. The problem with it is it places the responsibility for suffering on the victim instead of the perpetrator. Yes, sometimes we do suffer because of things that we inflict upon ourselves, but much of the suffering we experience in our lifetimes comes from the sins of other people. It's nice to think we can just sit back and eliminate suffering if we stop caring about everything, but it's unrealistic.

Suffering is an inevitable part of life. It's part of our world. Whether we want to hear it, it is also a part of being a Christian because it is a part of being a human being. Christians don't cease to live in this world, nor do they cease to be human beings with thoughts, feelings, ideas, and a fleshly body that is subject to injury and decay. As we go along, we are going to suffer at times. People don't always treat us right, we make our own mistakes, we go through periods of illness or physical discomfort, and sometimes stuff just happens that causes us to be uncomfortable, frustrated, anxious, stressed, or upset.

Romans 5:3-4:

Moreover [let us also be full of joy now!] let us exult and triumph in our troubles and rejoice in our sufferings, knowing that pressure and affliction and hardship produce patient and unswerving endurance. And endurance (fortitude) develops maturity of character (approved faith and tried integrity). And character [of this sort] produces [the habit of] joyful and confident hope of eternal salvation. (AMPC)

Job 42:1-6:

Then Job answered the LORD,
"I know that You can do everything
and that Your plans are unstoppable.

"You said, 'Who is this that belittles my advice
without having any knowledge about it?'
Yes, I have stated things I didn't understand,
things too mysterious for me to know.
"You said, 'Listen now, and I will speak.
I will ask You, and You will teach me.'
I had heard about You with my own ears,
but now I have seen You with my own eyes.
That is why I take back what I said,
and I sit in dust and ashes to show that I am sorry." (GW)

The reason suffering hasn't yet been eliminated is because sin has not yet been eliminated, either. It might not have the victory or the hold over us any longer, but it is still at work, in this world, through the movements of the evil one and those who do his bidding. If sin has not yet been eradicated, that means there are plenty of people the world over who still feel its effects. They need a hand up and a lasting hug to help them get to a place of healing. In other words, suffering produces powerful servants, which means suffering produces a deeper purpose. It helps us walk better with Christ, Who paid the ultimate price in suffering for our sins. Suffering brings us to a place of embracing salvation in a different way, thus reminding us of what it means to be a true servant.

Servanthood isn't something we pick up and put down at whim. We don't decide to be a servant one day, and the next, we stop because it gets too uncomfortable. From suffering we can rejoice, because in our discomforts we can be patient and enduring in and out of season. We aren't so easily wavering because we know we can live with anything or without it. The enemy loses that much more ground over control of our lives, and we gain that much more victory as we strive to be more like Christ. In greater pursuit of servanthood, we might be asked to give things up, change stuff in our lives, or shake some stuff up, but we can trust that all things work together for our good, because we love God and trust the calling according to His purpose, just like Job did.

Reflections

- How do you feel about men who have been victimized?

- What kind of friend are you? How can you be a better friend?

- What kind of friends do you have around you?

- Do you use money and things to substitute for giving of yourself? If so, what can you do to change this?

7
HOSEA: A MAN WHO SERVED BY LIVING THE IMPOSSIBLE

———————————×( )×———————————

THEREFORE, BEHOLD, I WILL ALLURE HER, AND BRING HER INTO THE WILDERNESS,
AND SPEAK COMFORTABLY UNTO HER.
(HOSEA 2:4, ASV)

- **Reading assignment:** The Book of Hosea

Men in church are told they should want to be strong like David, responsible like Boaz, handsome like Saul, loyal like Joseph, and wealthy like Solomon. We have our "favorites" when it comes to the Bible models we emulate. We don't ever stop to think that David was an adulterer, Boaz didn't want to marry Ruth, Saul was a big wuss, Joseph had every intention of abandoning Mary, and Solomon not only had too many wives, but he was also an idolater. When we talk about these men, we only talk about the attributes that we like in them, the characteristics that sound authoritative, bold and "manly." We like the idea of our men emulating the attitudes and characteristics of kings, leaders, and wealthy businessmen.

There's a man that we don't ever talk about, however. His characteristics are perhaps some of the most important for men (especially married men) to emulate. His name is Hosea, and he was a prophet with a mighty hard job to do.

Not only did he have to prophesy to Israel, but he also had to live the prophecy of Israel in his personal life. He challenges every man who is married, wants to get married, and every Christian who thinks they are called to examine if these are things any of us really want to pursue. His commitment, heart, love, and discipline despite the questions he surely must have had make us all step back and look at ourselves in a deeper way.

At the very heart of his ministry, Hosea was a servant. Before he was Prophet Hosea, husband Hosea, father Hosea, or Minister Hosea, he was a man, before God, who desired to serve above all things. His focus and service show us a powerful type of the ministry of the evangelist, whose main purpose is to make Christ known, manifesting His love every conceivable way possible. If there were more with the same commitment Hosea had, both marriage and the church would be mighty different.

Embracing the faith, even if no one else does

Over the past 25, years, the blame for men not wanting to attend church has gone to the women. As I mentioned earlier, the criticisms ranged from the intense to the sublime. They include everything from women leaders wanting to paint their sanctuaries pink to men not wanting to defer authority to women. Let's get a couple of things straight: it is absurd to blame women for men not wanting to attend church. Both the church herself and the Bible are feminine (the word for Scriptures is female), so if men are Christians, those are two female authorities they must accept if they are going to be serious as believers. If they can't accept female authority, they are going to have trouble embracing the life of the church and the spiritual authority that the Bible carries. As for women in leadership wanting to paint their sanctuaries pink, I would agree this is probably a little much and it probably wouldn't be a color I would consider for the walls of the church, but men go to work with pink walls and restaurants with pink walls and home with pink walls and bathrooms with pink walls, and I don't see it stopping them from going to those places and making themselves quite at home. As for too many women being present at church, there are also lots of women at strip clubs and brothels, but I don't see men refrain from going to those. (If anything, I would think that more women than men in a church would be a plus for men to attend!)

(I'm sure that you have figured out the old excuses we circulate aren't going to work with me.)

Men aren't going to church because they don't want to go. It has nothing to do with who is in the pulpit, what color the walls are, the smell of the potpourri in the bathroom, the ratio of men to women in the sanctuary, or the fact that they must wear something other than golf pants to service. Let's stop all that nonsense. Maybe instead of blaming women for the reasons men don't seem to go to church, we should consider the image we give of men in church is often unattainable for the average man. The concept of trying to live up to David, Solomon, Boaz, Old Testament Joseph, New Testament Joseph, Jacob, Abraham, or even Moses can seem intimidating and impossible. When the characteristics of these men are conflated without considering the counterbalances of their characters (the less positive qualities they had as human beings), the men seem impossible to emulate. It doesn't help the men who are selected as role models are often leaders of nations, warriors, perceived to be great with women (even though most of them weren't) and the ultimate "alpha men" that are thought most desirable.

Teaching only one side of any Biblical figure is wrong. Such causes us to think they were superhuman, one-dimensional people who never made mistakes, screwed up, or had feelings or difficulties. If we keep teaching men this is how they are supposed to be, they will never find themselves comfortable at church or with God. The bar has been set unreasonably high, and it is causing men to avoid going to church because they don't identify with the male figures portrayed in our clever pulpit renditions of Bible stories.

If we were to teach more balanced perspectives of

Bible men – and especially if we were to teach more about men in the Bible who were different, quiet, subdued, or sacrificial – I believe more men would be interested in attending church.

Enter the humble Hosea, just an ordinary guy with a great faith and a powerful heart. He wasn't a warrior or a ruler; he was a prophet, a servant of God who lived an ordinary life in an extraordinary way.

Hosea 1:2-9:

When the Lord began to speak through Hosea, the Lord said to him, "Go, marry a promiscuous woman and have children with her, for like an adulterous wife this land is guilty of unfaithfulness to the Lord." So he married Gomer daughter of Diblaim, and she conceived and bore him a son.

Then the Lord said to Hosea, "Call him Jezreel, because I will soon punish the house of Jehu for the massacre at Jezreel, and I will put an end to the kingdom of Israel. In that day I will break Israel's bow in the Valley of Jezreel."

Gomer conceived again and gave birth to a daughter. Then the Lord said to Hosea, "Call her Lo-Ruhamah (which means "not loved"), for I will no longer show love to Israel, that I should at all forgive them. Yet I will show love to Judah; and I will save them—not by bow, sword or battle, or by horses and horsemen, but I, the Lord their God, will save them."

After she had weaned Lo-Ruhamah, Gomer had another son. Then the Lord said, "Call him Lo-Ammi (which means "not My people"), for you are not My people, and I am not your God."

Hosea 3:1-5:

The Lord said to me, "Go, show your love to your wife again, though she is loved by another man and is an adulteress.

Love her as the Lord loves the Israelites, though they turn to other gods and love the sacred raisin cakes."

So I bought her for fifteen shekels of silver and about a homer and a lethek of barley. Then I told her, "You are to live with me many days; you must not be a prostitute or be intimate with any man, and I will behave the same way toward you."

For the Israelites will live many days without king or prince, without sacrifice or sacred stones, without ephod or household gods. Afterward the Israelites will return and seek the Lord their God and David their king. They will come trembling to the Lord and to his blessings in the last days.

Hosea was a prophet with a long story and an uncomfortable task. He was told by God to marry a prostitute, then have children with her, only for them to go their separate ways. She was off as a prostitute, living with another man, when God told Hosea to go and get her, and show her love and care, just as He would do to the nation of Israel. This loving care extended to Israel would eventually result in a remnant return unto the Lord, where God would settle those people and care for them Himself.

Let's rewind back to the first part of that story: here is Hosea, ordinary guy number one, told by God to go and break every conceivable law, ideal, and principle possible for a prophet: go and take a wife who was a prostitute and then have children with her. I don't know we can even fathom how difficult it must have been for Hosea to obey God, but we can trust for sure that if Hosea teaches us nothing else, he teaches us that obedience can be hard. Not every situation that goes against the grain is of the enemy (most are from God, believe it or not). This applies to family life as well as calling, and it means that our position is to rise instead of always assuming something that's different isn't right.

Which brings me to the point I made earlier about men going to church. Hosea proves that for a man to be a proper servant, he must embrace the faith for himself, even if his spouse or family does not. We hear all the time about women who stand in the faith and believe God for salvation for lost family members and who attend church even though their spouses and children are spiritually lost. Seldom do we hear about the reverse, even though Hosea really does prove that if a man is serious about God, he will persist in relationship with God and go to church whether his wife and children go, or not. Men can do the same thing that anyone else does when their spouses or children won't attend, and should do the same thing, whether the walls at the church are pink or there are a lot of women there. Going to church and persisting in a relationship with God has nothing to do with what everyone else around you want to do, but everything with recognizing that obedience to God is key. You must obey God for Him and for you. Yes, as in the case of Gomer and Hosea's kids, it did benefit them, but you can't believe in God for your spouse, your kids, or for everyone else – you have to believe and obey for yourself. The sooner you grab hold of that, the better servant you will be, no matter what everyone else around you is doing.

<u>Serving through your calling</u>

When I did an eight-part series on the Book of Hosea at Sanctuary Apostolic Fellowship (now Sanctuary International Fellowship Tabernacle – SIFT) in Raleigh, North Carolina in late 2015 and early 2016, one of the first things I noticed was the way Hosea's call as a prophet overlapped with his family life. In fact, the more I thought about it, most of the prophets in the Old Testament all had rather extraordinary circumstances in accompaniment of their calls. The reason for this: they didn't just preach a word detached from their own selves and lives. They also lived out their callings.

This should cause us to wake up and pay attention, especially with the rush of people who claim to be called to apostolic and prophetic ministry today. How many of them have unique, unconventional family situations or personal lives? I'm not talking about being on their fifth marriage in ten years or having a parade of children born out of wedlock as they sit in jail over child support arrears. I'm talking about how many of these people with callings have difficult marriages that they try to make work, despite the odds? How many of them personally experience the type of struggle and difficulty we see in church today? How many are there who are willing to marry someone whose life is less than ideal and won't create the perfect postcard image for the media to embrace?

If people are as much about families as they often claim to be, they should be willing to serve through their own lives than select marital partners and favor family members based on social image and perception. If someone truly has a message from God, they are going to live that message in their own lives. The truly called of God live a little different, perceive things in a different sort of way, and have a different sort of experience in their ministries.

Hosea 8:1-3:

"Put the trumpet to your lips!
 An eagle is over the house of the Lord
because the people have broken my covenant
 and rebelled against My law.
Israel cries out to Me,
 'Our God, we acknowledge you!'
But Israel has rejected what is good;
 an enemy will pursue him.

Hosea reminds us that if we are called of God, our first call is, above all, to be a servant. It's willing to go where God wants us to go, adopt the lives that God wants us to adopt, and follow His will unto the end, even if it is hard for us at times. Hosea's life had a greater purpose, which means his marriage and family life did, too. It wasn't about keeping up appearances, but about the salvation of a nation, which started with efforts to restore and show love and affection to his own immediate family.

Every single one of us has something we are called to do. Some people are called to work in ministry, and some people are called to work in the world, making money to live, support their families and the Kingdom of God. Figuring out that calling can be complicated but discerning where you are best suited and of use for God's service enhances your life and your outlook quite a bit. Yes, what God asked Hosea to do was hard, but his heart for service made it so answering that calling was that much less burdensome.

It's awesome to be called and discern that calling, especially in the beginning. I can vouch for how awesome it can be to be in God's service, as a minister, a business owner, and a wife. I also can't deny that knowing you are called to do something doesn't always make it easy, fun, or a breeze. Serving through a calling is still a service; it still takes effort and perseverance, sometimes when you want to do it the least.

Serving as a husband

Whenever I read about Jacob, Boaz, David, or the rest of them, I conclude they were men of great faith...but they weren't men I would want to marry. They might have loved God, but when it came to the women in their lives, most of these men had serious issues with fidelity. Boaz, the one who didn't seem to have that problem, wasn't the least bit interested in marrying Ruth, and she had to make all the moves on him. None of them represent a very good relationship balance. While I completely agree they were real human beings living in a different era than we do now...that doesn't make them any more appealing to me as men.

Jeremiah was a prophet who gives insight into being a man who was called to be single. He demonstrated that it was possible to serve God as a single man, and to do so with dignity and integrity. While there were other single men in the Bible, I believe Jeremiah demonstrated the single life in a way that some other single men did not do as well. If I had to pick a man in the Bible who I think would make a great husband, I would pick Hosea. Hosea showed his wife a commitment that was literally otherworldly: it came from

God's direction and touched his heart and his life in a way that we don't often see in marriage. Much of the world (and the church as well) gives us the impression that fidelity is impossible for men and they are the ones to get a wandering eye and stray when married. Hosea proves that being a faithful husband is possible and that being a good husband is more than just paying bills or coming home every night after work. Being a good husband is rooted in a sincere and deep love, first for God unto obedience, and second for her, recognizing what he has in her and in making her know just how important she is in his life.

Hosea 2:15-20:

There I will give her back her vineyards,
*   and will make the Valley of Achor a door of hope.*
There she will respond as in the days of her youth,
*   as in the day she came up out of Egypt.*

"In that day," declares the Lord,
*   "you will call Me 'my husband';*
*   you will no longer call Me 'my master.'*
I will remove the names of the Baals from her lips;
*   no longer will their names be invoked.*
In that day I will make a covenant for them
*   with the beasts of the field, the birds in the sky*
*   and the creatures that move along the ground.*
Bow and sword and battle
*   I will abolish from the land,*
*   so that all may lie down in safety.*
I will betroth you to Me forever;
*   I will betroth you in righteousness and justice,*
*   in love and compassion.*
I will betroth you in faithfulness,
*   and you will acknowledge the Lord.*

I could probably write an entire book on the relevance of servanthood in marriage, especially for men. The church puts so much emphasis on its errant viewpoint of women's roles in relationships that we don't talk a lot about what it takes to make a good husband and what men can do to improve their marriages. There are some powerful verses about men and marriage, and about just what marriage points to for men, but we often skip the part about the men and focus exclusively on the sections about the women.

Ephesians 5:25-33:

Husbands, love your wives, just as Christ loved the church and gave Himself up for her to make her holy, cleansing her by the washing with water through the word, and to present her to Himself as a radiant church, without stain or wrinkle or any other blemish, but holy and blameless. In this same way, husbands ought to love their wives as their own bodies. He who loves his wife loves himself. After all, no one ever hated their own body, but they feed and care for their body, just as Christ does the church— for we are members of his body. "For this reason a man will leave his father and mother and be united to his wife, and the two will become one flesh." This is a profound mystery—but I am talking about Christ and the church. However, each one of you also must love his wife as he loves himself, and the wife must respect her husband.

1 Peter 3:7:

Husbands, in the same way be considerate as you live with your wives, and treat them with respect as the weaker partner and as heirs with you of the gracious gift of life, so that nothing will hinder your prayers.

If in marriage a man is called to love his spouse as Christ loved the church, let's not minimize what the Bible teaches about marriage for men. Men are to sacrifice themselves for their spouses, rendering their own act of submission unto them. Just as Christ gave up His life, so men are to give up the parts of their lives that make them difficult, unfit for marital relationships (if they desire to be married). I can't think of a better Biblical example for this besides Hosea. Hosea shows us that to be a good husband, a man needs to have:

- **A solid prayer life:** We talked about the importance of prayer in a general sense when we looked at Job, but the value of prayer is worth repeating here. It is truly essential for marital life, as well. Men need the rooting of divine guidance to make marriage work and to tap into the needs, wants, desires, and care of their mates. To be a good husband, you need to have a good relationship with God.

- **Let God guide and speak to you about your relationship**: Hosea had to pay special attention to the words God spoke to him about Gomer. God's words about Gomer weren't always negative or punitive. He never told Hosea to treat her like a child or demean her, but to draw her with love and with kindness. God isn't going to encourage a negative or demeaning attitude in your marriage. Seek His guidance and insight during difficult times, and for ways to celebrate in the good times.

- **Making your spouse feel special and relevant:** I don't mean to imply that spouses of all genders don't need to grow up and accept that life happens, because we all do. Many of the bogus complaints couples have about relationships boil down to immaturity rooted in the fairy-tale ideas we bring into our marriages and intimate relationships. At the same time, balance is needed between making your spouse feel completely devalued and giving the impression that they are pampered royalty. This means: get a special gift every now and then for no special holiday or occasion, help out around the house, do things to help out so they have time to do something else (no strings attached), plan fun outings, spend time together, listen to them, hold them close at night, tell them how attractive they is to you, and let them know how important they is to you.

- **Forgiveness in marriage:** Forgiveness between Hosea and Gomer pushes an extreme most aren't comfortable exploring in their own lives. Yes, the purpose of that expression was to demonstrate God's love for His people, even when they were lost in deliberate sin and in spiritual rebellion. On the other hand, it shows the necessity of forgiveness in a marriage relationship. While most couples probably won't experience Hosea's same situation, they will encounter hurts, offenses, and opportunities where forgiveness is not only an option, but also a must. To be a good husband and a good father, you must know how to forgive.

<u>Expressing love</u>

1 Corinthians 13:4-7:

Love is patient and kind. Love is not jealous [envious], it does not brag, and it is not proud [arrogant; conceited; puffed up]. Love is not rude [disrespectful], is not selfish [self-serving], and does not get upset with others [is not easily provoked/angered]. Love does not count up [keep a record of] wrongs that have been done. Love takes no pleasure [does not rejoice] in evil [wrongdoing; injustice] but rejoices over the truth. Love patiently accepts all things [bears all things; or always protects], always trusts [believes all things], always hopes [hopes all things], and always endures [endures all things]. (EXB)

Hosea's relationship with Gomer proves that love is not selfish, just like we were always taught. Instead of making love about many of the things we make it about – trips, fancy weddings, expensive and elaborate gifts, huge parties – Hosea proves that love is about actions that are far more common and far more needed. Loving someone requires more than gifts, spending a lot of money, and big parties.

There is nothing wrong with big gestures, but relationships that move from gesture to gesture are doomed to failure. There needs to be substance in every relationship.

Hosea 2:21-23:

"In that day I will respond,"
declares the Lord—
"I will respond to the skies,
and they will respond to the earth;
and the earth will respond to the grain,
the new wine and the olive oil,
and they will respond to Jezreel.
I will plant her for myself in the land;
I will show my love to the one I called 'Not my loved one.'
I will say to those called 'Not my people,' 'You are My people';
and they will say, 'You are my God.'"

Every relationship needs a substance of love, expressed in a way that taps into the uniqueness of the relationship's specific needs. Hosea displays the need for a man to express his love for his spouse, even when they may seem unlovable. Love is not always easy and does not always come with a party or special occasion. Gomer needed love the most when she was the most unlovable. The same is true with us in our relationship with God, and the same is true with us in marriage. If you are going to be a married man or are already are one, there are going to be times when you have to step up to the plate and make that effort to express the love you have for your spouse, even if you are angry, having a hard time yourself, or you don't feel like it.

I'm sure that Hosea and Gomer separated because Hosea found himself in a place where he was tired of trying with her. He was disgusted with the situation, and understandably so. Yes, he was a prophet, but he was still a human being in a marriage that, from the outside looking in, seemed doomed to fail. Every person who reads this book has also had those feelings of frustration and anger at points in their intimate relationships. What Hosea proves to us is that if we want a relationship to work, those feelings of frustration must be broken down to discover true and abiding love, time and time again.

Hosea proves to us that relationships take effort to work. This is different from trying to work a relationship, which is something else entirely. If you are working all the time to keep a relationship afloat or to make a relationship work where there isn't a relationship, the efforts are fruitless. If you have a relationship you know is good or you know can be even better, it takes conscientious work to make sure that you contribute your part to the relationship. Your spouse should know you're on their side, wanting the best for them, believing for them, and encouraging them, no matter how difficult things are.

A word of caution on this: Hosea's purpose in marrying a prostitute, having children with her, and getting back together with her after divorce was due to his prophetic ministry. I don't want to give the impression that Hosea and Gomer's reconciliation is for every marriage or every situation. I also don't want us to get the idea that a man should always defer or chase a spouse in various marital situations. Just as it's wrong for a woman to always to defer to the man, it's also wrong for the man to always defer to his spouse. Don't think that Hosea teaches men to be without self-respect or identity. We don't have the specific dynamics of their everyday lives recorded in the Bible, and this is deliberate. Gomer and Hosea's marriage was for a bigger purpose, and that was to teach us about God's love for us and His pursuit of us, even if we are in sin and reject Him.

Serving as a father

Hosea's command to marry Gomer specifically included a clause to have children with her.

Hosea 1:2:

When the Lord began to speak through Hosea, the Lord said to him, "Go, marry a promiscuous woman and have children with her, for like an adulterous wife this land is guilty of unfaithfulness to the Lord."

Many wonder why he was called to serve in his marriage in this specific way. The reason had to do with the prophetic illustration God sent through Hosea's marriage to ancient Israel. If Gomer was a prostitute and actively involved as one either before or during the marriage, the paternity of the children would be in question. In ancient times, bridal prices for virgins were far higher than women who had already been married or sexually active because men wanted to ensure the children produced during a marriage were her husband's biological children. They didn't have paternity tests in those days. Not properly understanding much of reproductive science, if a woman ever had sex either before or during the marriage with another man, a husband had the right to question whether the children he raised were his. This might sound absurd to us today, but this type of understanding caused women to be killed, marriages to dissolve, and tension in households, even sometimes without justifiable cause. Thus, what Hosea was asked to do was definitely a servant's task...that nobody else wanted. He was called by God to raise children that he didn't even know for certain were his, and that must have caused some heavy conflict within his mind. Every time he called those kids by name; he was reminded of the prophecies to befall Israel. Calling them in from play reminded him of his difficult, problematic, and dysfunctional marriage. Circling back to the ultimate purpose, it reminded him of what he, as a prophet, was called to do.

Amid his difficulties, Hosea gives us insights into the servant's heart of a true father. When we think of Hosea, we automatically think of him as a husband and a prophet, but we don't think about his work with his children. To maintain his prophetic call, his relationship with his children must have been strained at times. Knowing the end of the prophecy, however, I do believe Hosea persevered and continued to demonstrate his love for his children.

How do I know this? God's heart toward His people and

His love for us are constant themes throughout the book of Hosea. Yes, Hosea and Gomer are the major players in terms of characters, but Hosea wasn't just called to have a wife; he was also called to have a family. The way that God relates to His people in Hosea is not just in the context of an intense love such as between spouses, but also as parent and child. Even though God recounts the many ways that Israel (His children) have sinned against Him, strayed from Him, and moved away from Him unto idolatry, God makes it clear that He can't bear to punish them as they deserve, according to the law that was in place under the Old Covenant.

Hosea 11:1-9:

When Israel was a child, I loved him,
and out of Egypt I called my son.
But the more they were called,
the more they went away from Me.
They sacrificed to the Baals
and they burned incense to images.
It was I who taught Ephraim to walk,
taking them by the arms;
but they did not realize
it was I Who healed them.
I led them with cords of human kindness,
with ties of love.
To them I was like one who lifts
a little child to the cheek,
and I bent down to feed them.

"Will they not return to Egypt
and will not Assyria rule over them
because they refuse to repent?
A sword will flash in their cities;
it will devour their false prophets
and put an end to their plans.
My people are determined to turn from Me.
Even though they call me God Most High,
I will by no means exalt them.

"How can I give you up, Ephraim?
How can I hand you over, Israel?
How can I treat you like Admah?
How can I make you like Zeboyim?
My heart is changed within Me;
all my compassion is aroused.
I will not carry out my fierce anger,
nor will I devastate Ephraim again.
For I am God, and not a man—
the Holy One among you.
I will not come against their cities.

Just as Hosea modeled God's love to Gomer, Hosea also modeled that love and forgiveness to his children. He raised them as his own, regardless of whether they were his biological children. He disciplined them, taught them the proper way, and prayed and encouraged them as people, even though they were a constant reminder of waywardness or the bigger spiritual problems that existed in Israel. These principles should be embraced by fathers of today if they want to be true servants. Being a parent requires a level of selflessness and sacrifice that can't be accomplished without a true servant's heart. When you decide to become a parent (or, if it was something that sort of "happened," when you decide to take responsibility) you set your mind to be involved in a child's life with the goal of raising a child through to adulthood. That means being understanding of the mistakes that come along, offering discipline as necessary, providing a constant sense of love and support, and making the point to be in that child's life: financially, spiritually, physically, and emotionally.

Hosea also proves to us that fatherhood is not just for biological fathers. As he raised children with a questionable paternity, this opens the door for stepfathers, foster fathers, adoptive fathers, spiritual fathers, mentors, and other men who step up to raise children who are not their biological children. The Bible proves that human biology doesn't always mean much to some people, and that while blood may be thicker than water, Spirit is always stronger than blood.

Serving as a separated or divorced man

When we think of Hosea, we think of a man who was called to bring about a reconciliation in his marriage because he was a prophet to Israel and was living out the prophecy in his personal life. A lot of people try to use Hosea to criticize people who get divorced, although this is not anywhere implied or stated in the Biblical text. To do so diminishes the relevance of what Hosea was instructed to do and takes the humanity out of Hosea's situation. We don't often realize that Hosea and Gomer were separated unto divorce during part of the Biblical story, because no one spends much time looking at that aspect of Hosea's walk.

Hosea 3:1-2:

The Lord said to me, "Go, show your love to your wife again, though she is loved by another man and is an adulteress. Love her as the Lord loves the Israelites, though they turn to other gods and love the sacred raisin cakes."

So I bought her for fifteen shekels of silver and about a homer and a lethek of barley.

Hosea and Gomer were separated unto divorce during part of their relationship. This separation provides us with a balance of ideals when it comes to intimate relationships and the decisions that we sometimes must make. Keeping in mind Hosea's and Gomer's relationship was for a purpose is an important bottom line to consider when dealing with the challenges of a relationship that isn't working. The fact that they divorced at all makes us aware that divorce does happen, it is sometimes necessary, and it doesn't mean the end for a man or woman of God. Whether or not someone winds up reconciling with a divorced spouse depends on the people involved in the situation. I would venture a couple needs to be called to do so, because trying to do something like that without God's intervention will quickly turn into a disaster.

What Hosea shows us, however, is that a divorced or separated man needs to carry himself with dignity. We talk a lot about women getting involved too soon after a divorce with another man or about dating around in public when they are still not legally divorced. Such conduct – announcing engagements while you are still married, blatant disrespect or mudslinging for your soon-to-be ex-spouse, or trying to place blame on someone else – are all behaviors that are disgraceful. They do not respect the personal dignity of a person who fell into a relationship that turned bad.

Whenever relationships end, all that any of us want is to prove that we're doing better than our ex. We want to seem like we have moved on first, that we weren't the reason the relationship went sour. Many think the answer to doing this is to sling mud, tell everyone what happened, maybe even exaggerate a little, all the while immediately looking for a new relationship to prove there's nothing wrong with us...but everything wrong with the other person. Even though we focus on women who behave like this, other genders (including men) do this as well, especially men who don't want to lose face and want others to feel their divorce wasn't their fault.

Hosea didn't immediately go out and find himself another wife, or even a date. He didn't try to prove that he didn't do anything wrong in the relationship. He waited out God's timing and direction on how to handle his relationship. He never spoke a bad or wayward word about Gomer. Hosea went on with his life, his ministry, and forward with his call. He sought God for whatever it was that he was supposed to do next.

If you are a divorced or separated man, take a lesson from Hosea. Trying to spread rumors, prove that you are ready to do something that you aren't ready to do, slinging mud or behaving unseemly, or rushing into a new relationship aren't the ways to handle a divorce. There is a time and a place for everything, and in the right time, divorced individuals can find the fulfillment they seek (including solid relationships) if they are only willing to be patient and trust in God.

Serving while waiting

Hosea's situation, though extreme, must have involved long periods of time that involved waiting. God told him to marry a prostitute, and he did...and then he waited. God told him to have children with Gomer, and he did...and then he waited. He was called to give a word, and then while he waited for the next word...he waited. In the meantime, he was attentive to his home situation, cared for his children as a single parent for a decent period, and waited for further instruction and direction.

Psalm 27:3-4:

One thing have I asked of the Lord, that will I seek, inquire for, and [insistently] require: that I may dwell in the house of the Lord [in His presence] all the days of my life, to behold and gaze upon the beauty [the sweet attractiveness and the delightful loveliness] of the Lord and to meditate, consider, and inquire in His temple. (AMPC)

Every time Hosea stepped up as a husband, father, provided a need for his family, gave a word to Israel, or waited for the existing spoken words to set in, Hosea was serving. He prayed while he waited, sought God's guidance at every turn, and had faith to endure as he went along in his life. Even though he might not be the most popular prophet in the Bible, he certainly was one of the most important. Hosea knew how to serve because he knew how to trust God with his life, even when that prophetic call took him down a road he would have never imagined before it all started.

Reflections

- Where are you with your faith life? Do you believe, even if no one else around you believes?

- How do you handle the hard things God asks you to do?

- How well do you serve in your marriage and family life? How can you serve better?

- How do you best express love? How can you express love better through service?

8

JESUS:
THE SAVIOR WHO SERVED US ALL

—————————————×( )×—————————————

AND HE SAT DOWN, AND CALLED THE TWELVE, AND SAITH UNTO THEM,
IF ANY MAN DESIRE TO BE FIRST, *THE SAME* SHALL BE LAST OF ALL, AND SERVANT OF ALL.
(MARK 9:35, KJV)

- **Reading assignment:** The Book of Matthew

This book wouldn't be complete if we didn't take the time to discuss the work of Jesus Christ in terms of His work as a servant. We like to talk about Jesus as our friend, our Savior, our Lord, and our constant companion, but we tend to get uncomfortable with talking about Jesus as a servant. I think this is for many reasons, the first one being there are many efforts to try and make the church seem more "masculine" to draw men to services. We see men such as the Apostles Peter or Paul as being "men," so we gravitate more toward their writings rather than looking at Jesus. It hasn't helped that many public figures denounce Jesus' teachings as "weak." Along with this mentality, people associate service with "women's activity." This is, of course, completely absurd, but is an intricate mind game leads many men away from service and from truly understanding the role that our Savior plays in our lives. Becoming the Savior of the world and laying down His life for us is the ultimate act of servanthood. It was done for a humanity that did not deserve it, that fell away from God and was in no way worthy of God's love manifest in the sacrifice of Christ. Regardless, this was exactly why it was done. It's precisely why Christ is the perfect model for us in serving others. He served us when we didn't deserve it, and we are called to serve in the same manner: even for those we feel don't deserve it.

It's hard for us to serve those we like; let alone those we don't like. Jesus makes it clear: if we are going to be Christian believers ("little Christs") that we, too, need to serve just as He did. This sounds nearly impossible if we level ourselves against Him, but not if we recognize He is at work within us. In this chapter, we are going to learn about setting back, letting Him take the lead in our lives, and allowing the Spirit to work within us and through us in all that we do.

Accepting the call to be counterculture

When you were a teenager, what were you? Were you a jock, a brain, a rebel, a cheerleader, or something else? Most of us didn't fit in with any of those classifications. Instead, we spent our time in junior high and high school trying to dodge those we perceived to be our mortal enemies. We might have had a few friends, but the average teenager wasn't the popular kid. We watched others be the center of attention, fussed over, followed, worshiped and adored, and part of us not only wondered why they got that treatment...we wondered why we didn't.

Those who were the focus of adoration probably demanded service from people to the point of slavery. They had other people buy them things, carry things for them, idolize them, want to be them, and make sure they maintained the most powerful social positions in the school. Maybe we wanted to be just like them, having that kind of power and prestige over others. Maybe we were afraid of them. Maybe some part of us wanted their control.

The people who were worshiped and adored back in high school were accepted by a greater culture. There might not have been anything special about them on the surface, but they likely had a worldly connection that merited them some sort of special treatment: a father who was a lawyer, a mother who was the socialite of the city, an older sibling who was the pride and joy of the school, a family with a long line of school graduates, or something else. Somewhere, someone in time had money, somebody gave money, and everyone from that family received special treatment in perpetuity because others felt indebted.

Fast-forward to today, the conformity train didn't stop when we were kids. If anything, there is just as much pressure to be one of the "cool kids" now as there was back then. Christians idolize big-time preachers with huge entourages clamoring to their every whim, as they are worshiped and adored by millions of people. They might have gotten where they are because of their predecessors or because they themselves have a lot of money, but no matter how you want to spin it…there they are. Admit it, especially for ministers, having that kind of fame under the guise of the Gospel is very intriguing.

We are intrigued with these people because we are doing what we did when we were young: we are measuring ourselves against them. Pastoring a church, being a good husband and father, being a great steward, doing volunteer work, and being committed to the Gospel doesn't sound as "important" as what the now cool adult kids are doing.

At some point in our lives, we must stop being so easily enamored with people who seem larger than life and seem to have it all. There is always going to be someone who seems to do it better than you, and you must learn how to be comfortable with that. Alpha male syndrome seeks to outdo, but there is a great peace in knowing that you are serving where you are supposed to, how you are supposed to, and when you are supposed to. Just because someone has a big ministry or a family life with photos, pictures, and successes everywhere doesn't mean they are living out Jesus' call, nor does it mean they are doing what He would have them to do.

Jesus was what we would classify as "counterculture." He was someone Who wasn't easily understood during His walk down here on earth. He wasn't trying to compete with other people, and He didn't care how much fame the Pharisees and Sadducees drew to themselves. It wasn't about everyone else or the spotlight to be cast, it was about leaving an impact on the world.

Philippians 2:5-11:

In your lives you must think and act like [have the same attitude as] Christ Jesus. [What follows may be from an early Christian hymn.]

Christ Himself was like God in everything [Who, being in the form of God].
    But He did not think that being equal with God was something to be used for His own benefit [or grasped; seized; held on to].
But He gave up His place with God and made Himself nothing [emptied Himself].
    He became like [took the form of] a servant [slave; bondservant]
    and was born as a man [in the likeness of humanity/men].
And when He was living [being found in appearance/likeness] as a man [human being],
    He humbled Himself and was fully obedient to God,
    even when that caused His [to the point of] death—death on a cross.
So God raised [exalted] Him to the highest place.
    God made His Name [or gave Him the Name] greater than [far above] every other name
so that every knee will bow to the Name of Jesus—
    everyone in heaven, on earth, and under the earth.
And everyone [every tongue] will confess that Jesus Christ is Lord
    and bring glory to God the Father. (EXB)

Being a servant isn't understood by most people. The majority of the world desires to be served but doesn't desire to serve. Servanthood isn't seen as a priority. When situations require it, most seek outside help to make sure they don't have to do the serving themselves. When you take on a true heart of servanthood yourself, it probably won't be understood well. You will be counterculture, somebody that does stuff nobody can explain, understand, and everybody will wonder why. You will become different in a way that will change you for the better and change the world around you, as well.

Setting the servanthood bar very high

It's fine for us to look to people in the Bible with admiration. There's no question that those who have gone before us in the faith faced hard trials and spiritual battles. It was their faith in God that pulled them through. They were warriors, lovers, leaders, fighters, and above all, believers, ordinary people who did extraordinary things because of their faith in God.

Just like we spoke of earlier, we need to be careful to avoid embracing Bible figures more than we embrace Jesus. Bible figures who were not Jesus were people just like us. Those people and faith in them cannot save us. They had their great models of servanthood, they had their ups and their successes, but every single one of them had serious downs, as well. They aren't unlike the pitfalls we experience, and that is the reason why they are in the Bible in the first place. God wants us to know that others have had the struggles that we do now, they did their best to overcome them, they struggled with their cultures (or sometimes drowned underneath them), and they still found a place of victory because of God. They aren't in there to make us feel bad about ourselves, compare ourselves to them, or to idolize them, thinking they have something better than we have now. Above all, Jesus is the One we are to aspire to be like, and we should aspire to develop His character within our lives.

Mark 10:35-45:

Then James and John, the sons of Zebedee, came to Him. "Teacher," they said, "we want you to do for us whatever we ask."

"What do you want me to do for you?" He asked.

They replied, "Let one of us sit at Your right and the other at Your left in Your glory."

"You don't know what you are asking," Jesus said. "Can you drink the cup I drink or be baptized with the baptism I am baptized with?"

"We can," they answered.

Jesus said to them, "You will drink the cup I drink and be baptized with the baptism I am baptized with, but to sit at My right or left is not for me to grant. These places belong to those for whom they have been prepared."

When the ten heard about this, they became indignant with James and John. Jesus called them together and said, "You know that those who are regarded as rulers of the Gentiles lord it over them, and their high officials exercise authority over them. Not so with you. Instead, whoever wants to become great among you must be your servant, and whoever wants to be first must be slave of all. For even the Son of Man did not come to be served, but to serve, and to give His life as a ransom for many."

Jesus was more than just a great man with some interesting teaching. As the Savior of the world, He set the bar high for us as to our conduct with others and the way we are to interact and care for one another. Instead of just being a surface-deep people, doing things to appease or appeal to other people, Jesus teaches us how to truly care about others in a way that changes and transforms ourselves. This is how we need to be if we want to be better servants.

The fact that He is a man Who is the greatest servant of all time is a true bonus, considering the content of this book. Even though women have historically served men, the greatest servant Who ever came into this world came as a man. He served other men, He served leaders, He served women, He served people who represent other genders, and He even served children. He proves to us, once and for all, that it is not only possible for men to serve but also required if they are to be a part of the Kingdom of God. That means all the protests that service is for girls, it's not sexually virile, and it's not what manly men do…just flew right out the window. If you want to be a real man, you need to be a counterculture man. That means you start serving, just as Jesus Christ taught you how to serve.

<u>More than surface deep</u>

Being a servant means adopting an entirely different thought pattern from what we embrace in the world. The world tells us we must be like the people we talked about earlier, and not wanting to be like them means the world just doesn't understand servants. The evidence of this is clear in the work of Jesus, Who spoke many things that people around Him did not understand. It's not that what Jesus taught was cryptic or hard to understand, it's that most people around Him didn't have the necessary thought and attitude to approach what He said with understanding.

John 6:60-71:

On hearing it, many of His disciples said, "This is a hard teaching. Who can accept it?"

Aware that His disciples were grumbling about this, Jesus said to them, "Does this offend you? Then what if you see the Son of Man ascend to where He was before! The Spirit gives life; the flesh counts for nothing. The words I have spoken to you—they are full of the Spirit and life. Yet there are some of you who do not believe." For Jesus had known from the beginning which of them did not believe and who would betray Him. He went on to say, "This is why I told you that no one can come to Me unless the Father has enabled them."

From this time many of His disciples turned back and no longer followed Him.

"You do not want to leave too, do you?" Jesus asked the Twelve.

Simon Peter answered Him, "Lord, to whom shall we go? You have the words of eternal life. We have come to believe and to know that you are the Holy One of God."

Then Jesus replied, "Have I not chosen you, the Twelve? Yet one of you is a devil!" (He meant Judas, the son of Simon Iscariot, who, though one of the Twelve, was later to betray him.)

Being a good servant isn't just a lot of talk, or even a lot of empty actions. I grew up in a church full of people who were all about service, service, service, but did it all with the wrong motives. If you want to be a good servant, you need to think like a servant. This means becoming more than just what might seem obvious on the surface. True servants of Jesus are also His disciples, and that means they are good students of the Scriptures and of all things related to faith. You don't have to have a theology degree to be a good disciple, but you do have to study long enough – and hard enough – to pass the servant test. You need to have a basic understanding of why we follow Jesus, why He is such an excellent servant, and how through growth and development we can find Him better through our own service.

Serving through humility

We often dislike service because we feel like we are serving people who don't "deserve" to be served. Think back, have you ever said one of these things or thought them (or maybe even heard someone else say them)?

- Homeless people just don't want to work.
- People on welfare are already taking all of my taxes; I am not doing anything else for them.
- Foreigners don't deserve to be in my country.
- Poor people are lazy.
- Women just want someone to pay their bills and take care of them.
- Rich people already have it all, they don't have to work for anything they have.
- Child support is all about women stealing money from men.

If you have ever made these types of statements, you weren't walking in humility when you said them. The root of these statements is pride, and pride is antithetical to humility. They are said by people in frustration, angry because they don't want to do what they know they are supposed to do. They've decided, for whatever reason, that someone else doesn't deserve it.

1 Corinthians 4:1-5:

This, then, is how you ought to regard us: as servants of Christ and as those entrusted with the mysteries God has revealed. Now it is required that those who have been given a trust must prove faithful. I care very little if I am judged by you or by any human court; indeed, I do not even judge myself. My conscience is clear, but that does not make me innocent. It is the Lord Who judges me. Therefore judge nothing before the appointed time; wait until the Lord comes. He will bring to light what is hidden in darkness and will expose the motives of the heart. At that time each will receive their praise from God.

If you are going to be a good servant, you can't classify people into the "deserving" or "undeserving" category. The very principle that Jesus Himself came to earth as a baby, grew to be a man, and then served humanity even though He wasn't like everyone else takes the "deserve" clause right out of serving. None of us deserved what Jesus did for us; we still don't, even if we make our best effort to live right. In the eyes of God, every single one of us is the "least" of these, unworthy of being in His presence due to sin. Because of what Jesus did for us, we are able to stand before the Father, without shame or embarrassment. That came about because of a servant's heart, because of Jesus' willingness to stand as reparation for our sins. Because of Him, we don't get what we might deserve.

In servanthood, we take the same posture and position that Jesus did, only we do it for others. We stop the "deserving" mindset and we just serve. We do the right thing, the needed thing, the purposeful thing, and we rise to the occasion instead of finding reasons not to do it.

Serving without judgment

One of my favorite passages in the Bible is Jesus' dialogue with the woman at the well, found in John 4:1-42.

Now Jesus learned that the Pharisees had heard that He was gaining and baptizing more disciples than John— although in fact it was not Jesus who baptized, but His disciples. So He left Judea and went back once more to Galilee.

Now He had to go through Samaria. So He came to a town in Samaria called Sychar, near the plot of ground Jacob had given to His son Joseph. Jacob's well was there, and Jesus, tired as He was from the journey, sat down by the well. It was about noon.

When a Samaritan woman came to draw water, Jesus said to her, "Will you give me a drink?" (His disciples had gone into the town to buy food.)

The Samaritan woman said to Him, "You are a Jew and I am a Samaritan woman. How can you ask me for a drink?" (For Jews do not associate with Samaritans.)

Jesus answered her, "If you knew the gift of God and Who it is that asks you for a drink, you would have asked Him and He would have given you living water."

"Sir," the woman said, "you have nothing to draw with and the well is deep. Where can you get this living water? Are you greater than our father Jacob, who gave us the well and drank from it himself, as did also his sons and his livestock?"

Jesus answered, "Everyone who drinks this water will be thirsty again, but whoever drinks the water I give them will never thirst. Indeed, the water I give them will become in them a spring of water welling up to eternal life."

The woman said to Him, "Sir, give me this water so that I won't get thirsty and have to keep coming here to draw water."

He told her, "Go, call your husband and come back."

"I have no husband," she replied.

Jesus said to her, "You are right when you say you have no husband. The fact is, you have had five husbands, and the man you now have is not your husband. What you have just said is quite true."

"Sir," the woman said, "I can see that You are a prophet. Our ancestors worshiped on this mountain, but you Jews claim that the place where we must worship is in Jerusalem."

"Woman," Jesus replied, "believe Me, a time is coming when you will worship the Father neither on this mountain nor in Jerusalem. You Samaritans worship what you do not know;

we worship what we do know, for salvation is from the Jews. Yet a time is coming and has now come when the true worshipers will worship the Father in the Spirit and in truth, for they are the kind of worshipers the Father seeks. God is spirit, and His worshipers must worship in the Spirit and in truth."

The woman said, "I know that Messiah" (called Christ) "is coming. When He comes, He will explain everything to us."

Then Jesus declared, "I, the one speaking to you—I am He."

Just then His disciples returned and were surprised to find Him talking with a woman. But no one asked, "What do you want?" or "Why are you talking with her?"

Then, leaving her water jar, the woman went back to the town and said to the people, "Come, see a man who told me everything I ever did. Could this be the Messiah?" They came out of the town and made their way toward Him.

Meanwhile His disciples urged Him, "Rabbi, eat something."

But He said to them, "I have food to eat that you know nothing about."

Then His disciples said to each other, "Could someone have brought Him food?"

"My food," said Jesus, "is to do the will of Him Who sent me and to finish His work. Don't you have a saying, 'It's still four months until harvest'? I tell you, open your eyes and look at the fields! They are ripe for harvest. Even now the one who reaps draws a wage and harvests a crop for eternal life, so that the sower and the reaper may be glad together. Thus the saying 'One sows and another reaps' is true. I sent you to reap what you have not worked for. Others have done the hard work, and you have reaped the benefits of their labor."

Many of the Samaritans from that town believed in Him because of the woman's testimony, "He told me everything I ever did." So when the Samaritans came to Him, they urged Him to stay with them, and He stayed two days. And because of His words many more became believers.

They said to the woman, "We no longer believe just because of what you said; now we have heard for ourselves, and we know that this man really is the Savior of the world."

The reason I like this story is because of the irony of what it has become. Somehow, we managed to take Jesus' longest dialogue with anyone in the Bible and turn it around to something it most definitely is not. If you have ever heard teaching on the woman at the well, it often stings of bitter judgment. I've heard of preachers calling her a harlot, a whore, a prostitute, an immoral woman, and even worse than that. They look down on her, shame her, and make her out to be something so unspeakable, you can't imagine why the Savior of the world even gave her the time of day.

Nowhere in the text does it say she was a prostitute, whore or harlot. She is never spoken of as being an immoral woman. It is very possible that given the customs of her day, she was within the bounds of moral law in terms of an engagement, living with a male relative, or something else. Given all these facts, she reports herself that Jesus told her everything that she ever did…not judge everything she ever did.

Jesus had the authority and right to judge her, if He so desired. Jesus told her everything she did; He didn't judge everything that she did. As perfect as He was, He was also love come down to earth, and chose not to judge her. Echoing the principle that mercy was better than sacrifice, He served her instead: with His listening ear, by ministering unto her, by offering her truth and a better way, and it changed her life. Instead of casting her off, Jesus offered her something more powerful: eternal life.

Every servant must put aside judgment and judgmental attitudes to be truly effective. This is hard for many men, because many are taught to be judgmental without even realizing it. Making quick decisions, not listening to all the details, skipping over essential facts, and being impulsive are all considered qualities of men that are just part of how they are. If you want to be a good servant, you are going to have to learn how to skip over snap judgments much of the time and listen to what people have to say. That way, you can gather proper information to make the right decisions and judgment calls.

Serving your enemies

We tend to have a cavalier attitude when it comes to those we classify as "enemies." Modern-day movements encourage us to avoid sticking around those who don't have our best interests at heart or who have ulterior motives. We quickly break ties and encourage others to do the same, even if all we have is a sinking feeling that something isn't right with that person. While I do not think it's wrong to distance yourself from someone who doesn't mean you well or is obviously out to destroy what God is trying to do, I don't think our desire to escape our enemies is as altruistic as it might seem. Underlying our desire to cut ties quickly and without any thought to the morrow is because we don't like the idea of being undercut and we dislike that we might have to suffer or go through something because of what someone else might do to us.

I believe there is a time and a place to distance ourselves from destructive fellowship. I also believe the Bible is quite clear in stating that there are certain character types that we should never unite with, no matter what our reasons might be. This is different, however, from accepting that there is a season to serve our enemies.

If you need a "selah pause" to think on that one, I understand. Take your time. Go scream in the pillow at the thought that if you are a true servant, you can even serve your enemies. I'll wait.

Matthew 10:1-4:

Jesus called His twelve disciples to Him and gave them authority to drive out impure spirits and to heal every disease and sickness.

These are the names of the twelve apostles: first, Simon (who is called Peter) and his brother Andrew; James son of Zebedee, and his brother John; Philip and Bartholomew; Thomas and Matthew the tax collector; James son of Alphaeus, and Thaddaeus; Simon the Zealot and Judas Iscariot, who betrayed Him.

Matthew 26:14-16:

Then one of the Twelve—the one called Judas Iscariot—went to the chief priests and asked, "What are you willing to give me if I deliver Him over to you?" So they counted out for him thirty pieces of silver. From then on Judas watched for an opportunity to hand Him over.

Matthew 26:21-25:

While they were eating, He said, "I can guarantee this truth: One of you is going to betray Me."

Feeling deeply hurt, they asked Him one by one, "You don't mean me, do You, Lord?"

Jesus answered, "Someone who has dipped his hand into the bowl with Me will betray Me. The Son of Man is going to die as the Scriptures say He will. But how horrible it will be for that person who betrays the Son of Man. It would have been better for that person if he had never been born."

Then Judas, who betrayed Him, asked, "You don't mean me, do you, Rabbi?"

"Yes, I do," Jesus replied. (GW)

Luke 22:47-48:

While He was still speaking a crowd came up, and the man who was called Judas, one of the Twelve, was leading them. He approached Jesus to kiss Him, but Jesus asked Him, "Judas, are you betraying the Son of Man with a kiss?"

John 12:3-6:

Then Mary took about a pint of pure nard, an expensive perfume; she poured it on Jesus' feet and wiped His feet with her hair. And the house was filled with the fragrance of the perfume.

But one of His disciples, Judas Iscariot, who was later to betray Him, objected, "Why wasn't this perfume sold and the money given to the poor? It was worth a year's wages." [6] He did not say this because he cared about the poor but because he was a thief; as keeper of the money bag, he used to help himself to what was put into it.

Judas was a serious enemy of Jesus Christ. He handed Him over to death out of his own greed. If we don't think that betraying Jesus ever occurred to Judas prior to selling Him out, we should think again. Judas was carefully watched and deliberately selected. There must have been something in his character and the way he interacted with Jesus that let the Pharisees and Sadducees know Judas was the man for the job. If the Pharisees and Sadducees could see this about Judas, what makes us think Jesus didn't?

All these facts, and Jesus never treated Judas differently. He received the same teaching and treatment as the rest of the disciples. He still went out, as an apostle, to do the work of the Lord earlier in time. and was even given the responsibility of serving as treasurer for the group! All the while, Jesus knew that Judas was going to betray Him!

Whether or not we like to accept this fact, Judas had a purpose, and he had a purpose even before he betrayed Jesus. Difficult or not, sense or not, knowledge or not, Judas served the purpose he was supposed to, in both the immediate and bigger picture. Jesus let him serve his purpose. Lesson for us who are learning about servanthood: the way we treat our enemies is just as important as how we treat our friends, if not more so.

I am also going to add a side note to this discussion specifically for leaders (although the principles can apply to anyone, especially anyone who administers governance of any sort). When in ministry, we tend to be trigger happy. Whenever someone gets distant, "funny," or quiet, we immediately run to someone else who will tell us that something isn't right about them, and they are becoming an enemy. This perceived paranoia causes us to lack discernment and to be quick to pull away from everyone and anyone, often without cause.

If we are called to be ministers, we are called to be servants not just to the world, but to the church, as well. This means we can't be so quick to disconnect all the time. Sometimes it's better to roll with the punches, as people say. If a disconnection must come, we should have ample evidence that someone has gone truly wayward, and we should disconnect with grace instead of the harsh, punitive treatments we see in many churches. I think it's fine when dealing with ministers to pull papers or disfellowship if it becomes necessary (those are governance issues, separate from servanthood), but we still need to remember our call to be servants. This means leaving the door open if someone reaches the point where they are ready to receive deliverance and knowledge, recognizing what is left and where they can find what they need.

A Christlike service

John 15:13:

The greatest love a person can show is to die for his friends [No one has greater love than this: to lay down one's life for one's friends; Jesus' death is the ultimate expression of this principle]. (EXB)

In servanthood, we are called to lay ourselves down for our neighbor. Jesus did it literally; we do it as we die to our flesh daily and continue to serve, using Him as our model. We live in a world where there is no shortage of need, no shortage of opportunities to serve, only lack of individuals who are willing to step up and do what needs to be done in service.

Matthew 25:31-46:

"The Son of Man will come again in His great glory [Dan. 7:13-14], with all His angels. He will be King and sit on His [sit on His] great [glorious] throne. All the nations of the world will be gathered before Him, and He will separate them into two groups [one from another] as a shepherd separates the sheep from the goats. The Son of Man will put the sheep on His right and the goats on His left.

"Then the King will say to the people on His right, 'Come, My Father has given you His blessing [those blessed by My Father]. Receive [Inherit] the Kingdom God has prepared for you since the world was made [from the creation/foundation of the world]. [For; Because] I was hungry, and you gave Me food. I was thirsty, and you gave Me something to drink. I was alone and away from home [a stranger], and you invited Me into your house [welcomed/received Me]. I was without clothes [naked], and you gave Me something to wear [clothed Me]. I was sick, and you cared for [visited; looked after] Me. I was in prison, and you visited [came to] Me.'

"Then the good [righteous] people will answer, 'Lord, when did we see You hungry and give You food, or thirsty and give You something to drink? When did we see You alone and away from home [a stranger] and invite You into our house [welcome/receive You]? When did we see You without clothes [naked] and give You something to wear [clothe You]? When did we see You sick or in prison and care for [come to] You?'

"Then the King will answer, 'I tell you the truth, anything you did for even the least of My people here [brothers (and sisters)], you also did for Me.'

"Then the King will say to those on His left, 'Go away [Depart] from me. You will be punished [are cursed]. Go into the fire that burns forever [eternal fire] that was prepared for the devil and his angels [the demons]. [For; Because] I was hungry, and You gave me nothing to eat. I was thirsty, and you gave me nothing to drink. I was alone and away from home [a stranger], and you did not invite me into your house [welcome/receive Me]. I was without clothes [naked], and you gave Me nothing to wear [did not clothe Me]. I was sick and in prison, and you did not care for [visit; look after] Me.'

"Then those people will answer, 'Lord, when did we see You hungry or thirsty or alone and away from home [a stranger] or without clothes [naked] or sick or in prison? When did we see these things and not help [serve; care for] You?'

"Then the King will answer, 'I tell you the truth, anything [to the extent] you refused to do for even the least of My people here [these], you refused to do for Me.'

"These people will go off to be punished forever [eternal punishment], but the good people [righteous] will go to live forever [to eternal life]." (EXB)

All the things we find in this passage are practical, everyday things each one of us can do if we are willing to exert a little effort. In my book, *Evangelism to Discipleship: Principles of Evangelism for the 21st Century* (Righteous Pen Publications, 2025) I break down the passage to explain it as follows:

- **I was hungry, and you gave Me something to eat:** The human body needs food. In alignment with our physical need, God has provided us plenty of natural resources to satisfy that need. It sounds simple enough, right? Unfortunately, wickedness controls and prevails in this world. That means those natural resources – God's provision for all of us – are usurped by evil people who use natural instincts (such as threat of hunger or famine) to manipulate others. The world has become a dominance game: the one who controls with the most resources "wins." This mindset is contrary to God's Kingdom. I agree Scripture teaches us to work for what we have (2 Thessalonians 3:10), but it's also wrong to expect people to work for wages that do not satisfy their most basic needs.

Feeding the hungry is seen in a literal sense – we should offer food to the hungry, providing food with health and nutrition in mind. This encompasses outreach, food banks, meals with a "message" (that include a service or preaching afterward), and distribution of food that would otherwise go to waste to those in need. It also requires us to stand for something deeper because food is a basic human need. Believing that Christians are called to give food to the hungry also means Christians should be opposed to political powers and programs that use starvation as a form of political control. Christians should believe in living wages, safe working conditions, and that people should have the opportunity to provide for themselves and their families without government interference.

It also means that we, as individuals, should be aware of how much we have and be willing to sacrifice every now and then so someone who doesn't have enough can have something. Whether you fast for world hunger and donate the cost of the food, focus on eliminating food waste, or become a more mindful consumer, being mindful with food is a witness to others.

- **I was thirsty, and you gave Me something to drink:** Our bodies are approximately 75% water. It only takes around three days for the body to dehydrate. Natural thirst is a type of spiritual thirst: finding the Living Water satisfies our spiritual longings (John 7:38). Since we understand this spiritually, we should also understand it practically. An individual without water or access to clean drinking water is a person in trouble. Millions die due to unsanitary drinking conditions. Not having access to clean water also means people are unable to bathe, clean clothes, cook food, and do a host of other things we take for granted every day.

   Being a Christian means providing drink to the thirsty along with food to the hungry. This covers all liquid nourishment, including other beverages (excluding alcohol). It also means supporting various charitable efforts to maintain and provide clean drinking water, pumps, wells, and other systems to those in need of such.

- **I was a stranger, and you invited Me in:** Ancient culture prided themselves on hospitality. It was considered downright rude to deny strangers lodging in one's home (Hebrews 13:2, 1 Peter 4:9) and provide shelter and nourishment during a visit. Inviting one as a stranger encompasses far more than inviting someone over for a few minutes or asking someone to come over – it was about being responsible for someone's basic needs while they were away from home and in another person's care. The wording of the passage indicates the need to see to care and provision for others beyond our own family – thus eroding any principle of nepotism that tends to bind and blind our world.

   We often don't consider ourselves accountable for others on this level. Yet anytime someone comes to visit at our request – be it for any matter, including spiritual – we are responsible for them. It's wrong to invite someone to something we host and then not take care of them, especially when someone travels to an area unfamiliar to them. Any time someone is coming somewhere at our request, we become responsible for them. It is wrong to invite someone to something, claiming to host an event, and then not take care of them – especially if the minister is travelling somewhere new or unfamiliar. This is especially true for church matters, when someone comes in for an event we host. Hospitality dictates they have suitable lodging, a place to rest, and offered the best we can give. It also relates to giving shelter to the homeless, through programs designed to aid such individuals in time of need.

In a more general context, giving shelter also applies to extending our borders beyond those we might find most familiar and comfortable. We can understand this in an obvious context – such as immigrants or foreigners – but I also believe we need to shrink issues down to a level of practical application. It's easy to allow those we know to be part of our inner circle and invite them to do things with us. It's a part of the Gospel to invite people to do things – to welcome in strangers – within our lives and our work. Our worlds should always be bigger than the minimal handful of people we see all the time. Yes, you can invite someone to go to church, but what about being somebody's friend? Have a meal with someone, talk to them, learn about them, and love them for who they are as a human being.

- **Naked, and you clothed Me:** Clothing has many purposes, from self-expression to a social statement. We focus more on the social statements of clothing than its practical purpose, thus forgetting practicality exists. Clothing is a form of shelter for the body against the elements of this world. Not having proper clothing can cause one to be too hot or cold, exposed to injury, or induce disease and illness. It's important that, as human beings, we have proper access to clothing because it protects the body and preserves it from foreign invasion.

Yes, we are commanded to clothe those who are physically naked and those unable to provide practical clothing for themselves through clothing drives and donations to organizations that provide inexpensive or free clothing to others. We should also be mindful of the clothing we buy, such as through programs that encourage Fair Trade or directly impact the lives of those part of an underdeveloped work force.

Many cultures recognize nakedness or lack of clothing as a source of shame. This means nakedness is also an image of shame or violation. By extension, this verse also reminds us to help, protect, and encourage those who have been violated or shamed through abuse in varied forms (including rape, sexual assault, domestic violence, gender or sexual discrimination, and mistreatment).

- **I was sick, and you visited Me:** Modern society has several means for sick patients: hospitals, doctors, nursing homes, extended care facilities, rehabilitation programs, and outpatient therapies. Things weren't this advanced, nor organized in ancient times. Illness was considered a curse for sin and, as a result, sick people were often considered untouchable. Not understanding germ theory, people feared disease could spread through moral failure and nominal contact with the terminally ill. This meant the sick were also regarded as a burden on families, as they were unable to work and earn their keep in physically demanding agrarian and textile societies. Chronic illness caused isolation, loneliness, familial rejection, and a life reduced to begging and poverty.

Visiting the sick serves as a ministry of healing by itself. It acknowledges the human element in healing, the basic need to interact with others in a compassionate and empathetic way. Today we can understand this as a need to visit the elderly, shut-ins, and those in hospitals and nursing homes, and even make a point to reach out to hospital patients. It also reminds us of the need to make ourselves available to others when someone is sick, whether temporarily or terminally. Bringing food or a gift, making a visit to help with laundry, cooking, or cleaning, or letting someone know you are thinking of them is vital to cure the wound of loneliness.

As a secondary point, visiting the sick calls to attention our own need to attend to both physical and mental health. We should always be advocates of physical and mental wellness, no matter what those two things look like for someone. This starts with our own efforts to break cycles, improve health of all sorts, respect neurodivergence, and socialize with others.

- **I was in prison, and you came to Me:** When I lived in Kentucky, people treated the county jail as the hotspot for ministry opportunity. There was a wait list to visit as a chaplain. Over thirty-five services per week were held in that tiny local jail. (Whether so many services were needed is another issue all together). Out of every place I've ever lived, that was the only one that had such an overwhelming response to prison outreach. Most of the time, prison ministry is treated as a non-existent, unimportant aspect of ministry life.

People often assume inmates deserve to be in prison, assuming they've done something both unpardonable and unforgivable. Historically speaking, prisoners have always been regarded as the lowest of the low. Ancient prisons were filled with political conquests (prisoners of war), thieves, debtors, or others guilty of other crimes (including religious confessions). Prisons were unsanitary, dangerous places, and inmates faced torture, violence, and brutal deaths.

Prison standards have changed in many countries, but not everywhere. There are still countries where jail conditions are overcrowded, unsanitary, and dangerous. Even in the best of conditions, prison – whether local, county, state, regional, or national – is an isolating and often terrifying experience.

Why would Jesus encourage us, as believers, to visit those in prison? Let us never forget Jesus Himself was tried and convicted as a criminal and was not guilty of any crime (John 18:38, Luke 23:4). We need to stop assuming everyone in prison is guilty, regardless of what a judicial process may produce. Not everyone who goes to prison is, in fact, guilty. Not everyone in prison is indignant to the crimes they have committed, nor is everyone a repeat offender. Sometimes things happen, whether planned or not, and people find themselves in situations we can never imagine for ourselves. In such a situation, we have no idea what we would do.

Visiting inmates is a humbling experience. It reminds us we are all sinners, and but for the grace of God are we here, today. Supporting prisoners reminds us that it's difficult to be bound to a "justice system" that's not always just, whether someone is there of their own doing, or not. God wants us to remember that forgiveness exists, no matter the circumstance behind an offense.

By extension, we are to remember those who are imprisoned by any host of issues, problems, or situations that keep them bound. As Christians, we are called to proclaim freedom to the captives (Isaiah 61:1). Whether a person is bound by the law (imprisonment) or by physical, emotional, mental, or addictive issues, we can still reach out to them with true liberty and love.

It's obvious that there's no shortage of possible opportunities to serve. Christians remain in this world, not to control or dominate it, but to serve it. We shouldn't be competing with the world but doing the necessary work to show people the love of Christ. As He lives within us, we have the power to represent Him while we are here.

We can't claim to believe in Christ and then not do the things He did (or at the very least, the things He tells us to do). Believing in Christ means doing what Christ did and what He calls us to do, right down to the present day. If we desire to remain worthy of the name "Christian," we better get started. This chapter outlines some great places to start. Which speak loudest to your call to serve?

Reflections

- Do you feel serving others makes you less of a man? Why or why not?

- When you think of famous Christians or preachers, how does it make you feel about what you are doing?

- Why should we aspire to be like Christ, more than anyone else in the Bible?

- What can we learn from Christ's treatment of Judas?

How should we, in turn, treat our enemies?

- Looking at the different suggestions for service in the book, which do you intend to try?

- What are some other forms of service you seek to adopt to become more Christlike in your character and actions?

9
THE APOSTLES PETER, PAUL, AND JOHN: LIVING FOR SERVANTHOOD

―――――――――――――――――――×( )×―――――――――――――――――――

LET NO ONE THEN SEEK HIS OWN GOOD *AND* ADVANTAGE *AND* PROFIT,
BUT [RATHER] EACH ONE OF THE OTHER [LET HIM SEEK THE WELFARE OF HIS NEIGHBOR].
(1 CORINTHIANS 10:24, AMPC)

- **Reading assignment:** The Book of 1 and 2 Corinthians, 1 and 2 Peter, and 1, 2, and 3 John

When I think of two Bible alpha males, I immediately think of the Apostles Peter and Paul. Peter was a political Zealot, he cut off another man's ear, and he was overly passionate about his views. He was eager to share those views with other people. He knew what he believed (to the best of what he had been taught) and was willing to go out on a limb for those beliefs. Of all things, he was a fisherman by trade, which meant he threw around and pulled around full, heavy nets, working off the sea, for his entire life. Paul was a tentmaker by trade, working with his hands in a trade full of heavy fabrics. He was an intellectual, a scholar, but also someone who wasn't afraid to get his hands dirty, jumping full in on killing those he felt were a threat to the orthodoxy of his faith. He was the epitome of power, of the execution of the law, and of doing what he

193

felt needed to be done.

Then there was the Apostle John, who was far quieter by his nature. He was known as the "apostle whom Jesus loved" and even artwork depicts him as being effeminate in his appearance and quiet in his demeanor. He might not have been the apostle who was voted most likely to jump out of an airplane or to conquer the Roman government, but he had a revelation of Who Jesus was and how important Jesus was long before the other two had any clue. He didn't betray or deny Jesus, and he was present with Him right up to His death.

The three apostles we are going to look at in this chapter were all different men, although Peter and Paul had more in common personality-wise with each other than either of them had with John. Despite their differences, they all had one very important thing in common: they were all men who were transformed by servanthood. They made a commitment to see this thing through and to walk it through to the very end, no matter how hard it was. Through their writings, we can see their ups and downs, their difficulties and their call, and why servanthood was so important to them – and to all men, right down to today.

Being good examples

I think that, deep down, one of the major things that motivated the early apostles in their work was the desire to be a good example. These were men who experienced a major transformation in their lives, and they wanted to show the world their transformation was genuine. They weren't bored with church, although they certainly grew tired of dealing with the same problems in other people, repeatedly. They knew the value in modeling proper behavior. If they were going to convince others that God was real, they had to produce a change in themselves first.

Being a good example is one of the first – and best ways – we can serve others. It's something we don't often think about, because it requires us to be very self-aware and self-conscious of our actions and interactions. We'd rather do some community service and leave it there when we are done with it. Yet being a good example is exactly what ensures that we, as Christians, have the continuous mindset of service. It's easy to do things without any connection to them, but it takes a conscientious effort to make sure what we do is done properly, and with proper meaning.

I had mentioned in an earlier chapter that I grew up in a church that valued service. There is nothing wrong with valuing service, but there was a major problem with how the message was translated to the people in the church. We were a church full of people who were quick to do things, but they were often done begrudgingly, angrily, with a wrong heart, and wrong motive. Anytime anyone questioned something about someone, they were quick to throw whatever it was they did up in their faces, as if they were more pious or better than someone else. They knew how to do things to be noticed, but they didn't know how to genuinely serve other people, without condition and without keeping score. Their actions were one thing, but their hearts remained unchanged.

John 13:15:

I have set you an example that you should do as I have done for you.

Philippians 3:17:

Join together in following my example, brothers and sisters, and just as you have us as a model, keep your eyes on those who live as we do.

1 Timothy 4:12-13:

Let no one despise or think less of you because of your youth, but be an example (pattern) for the believers in speech, in conduct, in love, in faith, and in purity. Till I come, devote yourself to [public and private] reading, to exhortation (preaching and personal appeals), and to teaching and instilling doctrine. (AMPC)

Titus 2:1-2,6-8:

You, however, must teach what is appropriate to sound doctrine. Teach the older men to be temperate, worthy of respect, self-controlled, and sound in faith, in love and in endurance.... Similarly, encourage the young men to be self-controlled. In everything set them an example by doing what is good. In your teaching show integrity, seriousness and soundness of speech that cannot be condemned, so that those who oppose you may be ashamed because they have nothing bad to say about us.

1 Peter 2:12:

Live such good lives among the pagans that, though they accuse you of doing wrong, they may see your good deeds and glorify God on the day he visits us.

Believers aren't called to just talk the talk and not walk the walk. This is especially true when it comes to those who are quick to talk much about the Christian life to others. Sure, we are all a little too free with our advice and especially our opinions...and step back and think about that for a few moments. Some of the most public, boisterous, and opinionated men of our era have been preachers, and they haven't been opinionated in a good way. They have set the stage that so many men (and individuals of other genders alike) feel the need to follow suit in with the same type of overly opinionated, rude, and blusterous attitudes that make other people feel silenced, checked, and demeaned. It only makes it worse that these attitudes are frequently expressed in the name of the "Bible." Rather than focusing on how we live our faith and living it in a practical and applicable way, the emphasis is for preachers to be show-stoppers; people who are known for their opinions rather than their beliefs, and for a misguided concept of being "old-fashioned" rather than examining how their beliefs can be relevant for the times.

<u>Serving with a change of heart</u>

If we think about the writings of the Apostles Peter and Paul, we see the transformation of individuals from worldly men with worldly approaches to problems and worldly attitudes into men who were spiritually minded and focused on things related to God. I'm leaving John out of this section (we will look at him by himself momentarily) because from what we have of John, his mindset and viewpoints were always spiritual, so those viewpoints were enhanced and transformed into a greater sense of truth. Even though both men were the quintessential alpha males as we would understand it, they had to walk away from those images and lifestyles to become what Jesus desired them to be.

The alpha male attitude is the opposite of humble servanthood. We see this fact nowhere better than in the characteristics of Peter and Paul prior to their work as apostles. Let's look at some of the characteristics and attitudes that the Apostles Peter and Paul had in their nature prior to their spiritual transformation to servanthood:

- **Peter:** Self-confident, avoided suffering, violent, aggressive, zealot-like behavior, denial, vengeful

- **Paul:** Arrogant, murderer, judgmental, vengeful, angry, misused authority, aggressive, hostile, intolerant

Let's now contrast those with the themes that they often spoke of in their writings: love, peace, submission, humility, joy, self-discipline, spiritual focus, and proper conduct. No more were they the men who lived out of aggression and dominance, because they found a better way that would change their lives and the lives of others, if they would allow God to work within them.

Romans 12:10:

Be devoted to one another in love. Honor one another above yourselves.

Romans 13:1:

Let everyone be subject to the governing authorities, for there is no authority except that which God has established. The authorities that exist have been established by God.

Romans 13:10:

Love does no harm to a neighbor. Therefore love is the fulfillment of the law.

1 Corinthians 13:4-7:

Love is patient, love is kind. It does not envy, it does not boast, it is not proud. It does not dishonor others, it is not self-seeking, it is not easily angered, it keeps no record of wrongs. Love does not delight in evil but rejoices with the truth. It always protects, always trusts, always hopes, always perseveres.

1 Corinthians 16:14:

Do everything in love.

Ephesians 5:21:

Submit to one another out of reverence for Christ.

Colossians 2:10:

And in Christ you have been brought to fullness. He is the head over every power and authority.

1 Peter 4:8:

Above all, love each other deeply, because love covers over a multitude of sins.

1 Peter 5:5:

In the same way, you who are younger, submit yourselves to your elders. All of you, clothe yourselves with humility toward one another, because,

"God opposes the proud
but shows favor to the humble."

The topics that the Apostles Peter and Paul wrote about reflect far more than just a desire to change and do something else. They reflect transformation, the passing from the old man to the new, becoming someone – and something – else entirely. Sometimes in these writings we see how difficult it was for them to transform, and at other times, we see how awesome it was for them to overcome. In both areas, we see just how important this transformation is, and that it is impossible to truly serve without it.

The brutish nature that many men display when they act as Peter and Paul did pre-salvation is one that makes a man difficult to deal with, difficult to tolerate, and unlovable to a partner who needs a godly man to love. It puts a man on a collision course toward personal destruction as he causes trouble rather than knowing how to handle it. Men who act like this aren't acting as grown adult men, but rather, as children high on too much testosterone. A true man – a truly attractive man – a truly godly man – knows the value of being a servant and in displaying and putting on that spiritual nature. It doesn't mean he never has moments where he could do better and it certainly doesn't mean he is perfect all the time, but it does mean that he aspires to be Christ-like in his character and have the attitude of what he can do for others and what he can do to diffuse negative situations as he goes through his life.

That means as a man, you are no less of what God will have you to be if you adopt a servant's nature. If anything, you are putting on the nature of Christ, which makes you more of a man. It will make it better for you to be around, it will make your relationships better, and it will make your ability to handle situations less inflammatory and more purposeful, because Christ will have the ability to move through you.

Serving with a spiritual heart

When I think of the Apostle John, I think about what life must have been like for him as a kid. I wonder about this because John always seemed to be different from the other apostles and disciples. He knew Who Jesus was from early on and knew where he needed to be: close to the Lord. He strikes me as being a little more on the quiet side than the others, enjoying the hours of hearing Jesus' teachings and embracing them, close to his heart, as he heard the words that made sense to him and finally set him free. Even though we have raised John's status to that of some sort of super-human being, John was still an ordinary human being with the same hopes and aspirations of most people: he wanted to be normal...yet he probably was never "normal." If he was as spiritual as a kid as he was as an adult, he probably spent most of his life misunderstood. I know how that goes, as I have struggled with the feeling that people just don't understand me and often just don't try, for whatever their reason may be. I've watched other people make that effort to understand the people in their lives and rise to a level where even if they don't really understand they still love them, only to wonder why people don't seem to make that effort with me...and I know John probably had the same thoughts. John probably got picked on, teased, was the butt of one too many jokes, and just wanted to have that feeling of knowing what it was like to fit in with other people and experience the acceptance that every human being seeks to have. I'd venture he probably had a hard time in his relationships and even a hard time in the arena of his faith, because he just wasn't on the same page as everyone else.

John was different. John was unique. Now, we love John. I have the distinct feeling that John didn't feel that from many sources in his life, and that it was probably hard for him as he watched the more macho guys in his life succeed as he felt left out.

Being misunderstood is hard. It is especially hard when everyone else around you try to turn you into someone or something other than what you are. I am sure that people told him he wasn't man enough because he didn't want to do what other guys did or behave like them. He was probably the nice guy who got dumped for the macho brute who beat his girlfriend, yet he was always there to listen. People told him he was weak, a floor-mat, and that he would never be anything the way he was.

Shame on them. Shame on everyone who tries to turn a sensitive boy or man into someone else and thinks that by being mean or intimidating, they will accomplish that. There is nothing wrong with a boy or a man being quiet, being loving, being attentive to the people in his life, being sensitive, or being artistic. Anyone who has anything to say otherwise ought to consult God, Who we call Father, Who created this entire world we see and is sensitive and caring to our every need and our every cry. There's nothing wrong with sensitivity or difference. There is something wrong with brutish intimidation and bullying because we dislike differences.

John 3:16:

For God so loved the world that he gave his one and only Son, that whoever believes in him shall not perish but have eternal life.

John 13:23:

One of them, the disciple whom Jesus loved, was reclining next to Him.

John 14:23:

Jesus replied, "Anyone who loves Me will obey My teaching. My Father will love them, and we will come to them and make our home with them.

John 20:2:

So she came running to Simon Peter and the other disciple, the one Jesus loved, and said, "They have taken the Lord out of the tomb, and we don't know where they have put Him!"

1 John 3:1:

See what great love the Father has lavished on us, that we should be called children of God! And that is what we are! The reason the world does not know us is that it did not know Him.

1 John 3:16-18:

This is how we know what love is: Jesus Christ laid down His life for us. And we ought to lay down our lives for our brothers and sisters. If anyone has material possessions and sees a brother or sister in need but has no pity on them, how can the love of God be in that person? Dear children, let us not love with words or speech but with actions and in truth.

1 John 4:7-21:

Dear friends, let us love one another, for love comes from God. Everyone who loves has been born of God and knows God. Whoever does not love does not know God, because God is love. This is how God showed his love among us: He sent His one and only Son into the world that we might live through Him. This is love: not that we loved God, but that He loved us and sent His Son as an atoning sacrifice for our sins. Dear friends, since God so loved us, we also ought to love one another. No one has ever seen God; but if we love one another, God lives in us and His love is made complete in us.

This is how we know that we live in Him and He in us: He has given us of His Spirit. And we have seen and testify that the Father has sent His Son to be the Savior of the world. If anyone acknowledges that Jesus is the Son of God, God lives in them and they in God. And so we know and rely on the love God has for us.

God is love. Whoever lives in love lives in God, and God in them. This is how love is made complete among us so that we will have confidence on the day of judgment: In this world we are like Jesus. There is no fear in love. But perfect love drives out fear, because fear has to do with punishment. The one who fears is not made perfect in love.

We love because He first loved us. Whoever claims to love God yet hates a brother or sister is a liar. For whoever does not love their brother and sister, whom they have seen, cannot love God, whom they have not seen. And He has given us this command: Anyone who loves God must also love their brother and sister.

It was probably easier for John to adapt a servant's heart. By his nature, he was that much farther ahead of the others. While he had an easier time accepting the servant's nature because it fit who he was as a person, it doesn't erase all the years he had to accept he was someone without a culturally accepted identity.

Even in finding his niche as a servant and specifically a servant serving as an apostle, I believe John still dealt with the feeling of not being "normal." The struggles that his colleagues had weren't ones he experienced, and he probably still had times in his life when he wished his identity wasn't so bound to who he was. He would still have times when he wondered what life would be like if he was different, and he probably had many days when he cried out to God in disbelief. He didn't understand why people were the way they were any more than they understood him, and living with that difference can be a difficult task, even when serving comes easier.

To all those men who follow in the Apostle John's footsteps: there's nothing wrong with you or with the way you are. You are as you are because God has made you that way and the way you are is both encouraging and amazing. There is no wrong way to be a man, because God calls each of us to be different and embrace our uniqueness. To all those who aren't like the Apostle John, but might resemble more of a Paul or Peter, don't give those who are different from you such a hard time. Learn from the insights that more sensitive and different men have and embrace some of those characteristics in your own walk of servanthood.

Serving with the times

I think one of the biggest challenges the church faces right now is the difficulty of remaining current rather than relying on old traditions to stay comfortable. Think, for a moment, about the way church tends to approach modern issues. Our answers tend to be rather monotone, all with the underlying expectation that we should "return" to something. The things we are trying to get people to return to aren't the Lord, but the activities and church stylings of former times. For example: we hear a lot of people talk about things such as tent revivals, holiness meetings, or convocation assemblies, and the need to return to such things. In and of themselves, these things aren't good or bad; they were simply things that have been done over the past 200 years by churches as outreach forums or ways to keep denominations informed and current. The problem with these activities is that if we rate their effectiveness in drawing in church members or maintaining them, they are severely on the downturn. As great as they might have been in days past and as nostalgic as they might make us today, they aren't things that are effective in reaching and maintaining members in our current atmosphere.

We don't live in an era of tent revivals, holiness meetings, or convocation assemblies. They were things that worked for a while, but in the scope of church history, have only been done for short periods of time. None of these events are found anywhere in the Bible (at least not in the context we now use them), and while I do not mean to suggest there is something unbiblical about them (there isn't), there isn't anything anymore Biblical about them versus us discovering a different way to reach out to our congregations and to society at large. What they have become are traditions, things we hold onto in the hopes that if we bring it back, it'll facilitate a nostalgic feeling rather than being effective in the long-term goal.

We have three choices when it comes to addressing changing times. The first option is to complain, making the decision to change one of choosing God or progress. This is a misnomer, because God is a good God, and the Holy Spirit is guiding us toward our ultimate progress as people. God doesn't change, but He does expect that we will change. We can't expect to revert to things that no longer work and hope that will change. The second option is to abandon truth and follow societal change, wherever it leads. This is also a bad option. While God doesn't expect we never abandon change, we also should never abandon truth. The third option is to embrace change is needed in the way the message is delivered, without contradicting or damaging the message. That is precisely what we need to do – adjust how we deliver the message to the era we are in now – while trusting that the Holy Ghost is what keeps the message alive and current down through the ages.

1 Corinthians 11:2-16:

I praise you for remembering me in everything and for holding to the traditions just as I passed them on to you. But I want you to realize that the head of every man is Christ, and the head of the woman is man, and the head of Christ is God. Every man who prays or prophesies with his head covered dishonors his head. But every woman who prays or prophesies with her head uncovered dishonors her head—it is the same as having her head shaved. For if a woman does not cover her head, she might as well have her hair cut off; but if it is a disgrace for a woman to have her hair cut off or her head shaved, then she should cover her head. A man ought not to cover his head, since he is the image and glory of God; but woman is the glory of man. For man did not come from woman, but woman from man; neither was man created for woman, but woman for man. It is for this reason that a woman ought to have authority over her own head, because of the angels. Nevertheless, in the Lord woman is not independent of man, nor is man independent of woman. For as woman came from man, so also man is born of woman. But everything comes from God.

Judge for yourselves: Is it proper for a woman to pray to God with her head uncovered? Does not the very nature of things teach you that if a man has long hair, it is a disgrace to him, but that if a woman has long hair, it is her glory? For long hair is given to her as a covering. If anyone wants to be contentious about this, we have no other practice—nor do the churches of God.

1 Corinthians 14:34-35:

Women should remain silent in the churches. They are not allowed to speak, but must be in submission, as the law says. If they want to inquire about something, they should ask their own husbands at home; for it is disgraceful for a woman to speak in the church.

1 Peter 2:18-21:

Slaves, in reverent fear of God submit yourselves to your masters, not only to those who are good and considerate, but also to those who are harsh. For it is commendable if someone bears up under the pain of unjust suffering because they are conscious of God. But how is it to your credit if you receive a beating for doing wrong and endure it? But if you suffer for doing good and you endure it, this is commendable before God. To this you were called, because Christ suffered for you, leaving you an example, that you should follow in His steps.

3 John 1:9-12:

I wrote to the church, but Diotrephes, who loves to be first, will not welcome us. So when I come, I will call attention to what he is doing, spreading malicious nonsense about us. Not satisfied with that, he even refuses to welcome other believers. He also stops those who want to do so and puts them out of the church.

Dear friend, do not imitate what is evil but what is good. Anyone who does what is good is from God. Anyone who does what is evil has not seen God. Demetrius is well spoken of by everyone—and even by the truth itself. We also speak well of him, and you know that our testimony is true.

The Apostles Peter, Paul, and John all dealt with traditions. They lived in a time where ideas, concepts, and the world they knew was rapidly changing. It didn't matter what those changes were, but it mattered they stayed current within the times when they lived. In fact, as we can see above, a lot of the advice they gave related to cultural differences, trends, and the times in which they lived.

The Bible doesn't fail to make provision for the fact that times were going to change. Surely we can all agree that the Apostle Paul was not advising women to wear head coverings if it was inappropriate for their time and era, or encouraging women to maintain a social status similar to property if society elevated above it, or that we should always have slaves for all time, or that men were always the most qualified people to teach in every situation between here and eternity. When we refuse to understand the Bible in a context that applies in the here and now, we are doing injustice to our perspectives about service and worldview.

The early apostles knew the only way they could serve those who were going through such rapid change was to serve them in ways that they would understand. This is, in large part, why they were so successful. They weren't trying to get people to back-peddle to an earlier time or to do something that didn't even work once upon a time. They knew the times in which they lived, they were educated for their day and age, and they used means and methods around them to convey their essential and life-saving Gospel message to the masses.

Sure, we don't like what everyone does. I am sure this is also a universal principle that's not new. We also don't always like the changes we face, especially when we find them a culture shock, something that shakes us to remember life isn't like we remember it and certainly not what it used to be. Just as the early apostles recognized life isn't what it used to be, this side of heaven, in this time, we aren't returning to any previous era of history. All we can do is move forward and know what is going on around us so we can identify the most effective to serve right now. We must find the eternal balance between change and truth, between modifying the method and presenting the eternal truth. If we approach evangelism and outreach like this, we will see our churches grow in relevance and find we don't miss our members. They will stop slipping through our communicative cracks.

Men serving as ministers

It's important to recognize the men who spoke words about leaders in the New Testament were men writing primarily to other men. While I firmly believe women were in leadership positions in the New Testament, I don't believe that, due to cultural perceptions, they were the majority. That's not to nullify their contributions or to say the words didn't apply to women, but they weren't always written with the female minority in mind. When they wrote letters discussing the important topics we like to avoid today: avoiding greed, maintaining personal integrity, loving their flock, maintaining their home lives, and reminders about living the Christian life were written to affect the lives of Christian male leaders (as much as leaders of other genders). Thus, male leaders need to take note of what men are called to do as ministers and how they are called to live. None of the early apostles were passive when it came to advice for leaders, and they were not subtle when it came to reprimands for improper conduct or behavior that was not befitting a servant of God and His people.

There has never been a question as to whether men are fit for service in ministry. If anything, it has been a position that men have filled, whether the man filling that position was called or competent for it...or not. History is full of men who were a disgrace to the offices they held. For whatever the situation might have been, they were allowed to continue in those positions. Being given a position because someone is a man isn't enough of a qualification, and the Bible does clarify that. It also doesn't mean a man should automatically have the highest position in a church or ministry, or that women (or people of other genders) can't cover men as their spiritual leaders. It means that just like anyone of any other gender needs to be called and qualified, so does a man, and that his qualification shows in the fruit that comes forth from that ministry work.

2 Corinthians 3:6:

He has made us competent as ministers of a new covenant—not of the letter but of the Spirit; for the letter kills, but the Spirit gives life.

1 Timothy 3:1-13:

Here is a trustworthy saying: Whoever aspires to be an overseer desires a noble task. Now the overseer is to be above reproach, faithful to his wife, temperate, self-controlled, respectable, hospitable, able to teach, not given to drunkenness, not violent but gentle, not quarrelsome, not a lover of money. He must manage his own family well and see that his children obey him, and he must do so in a manner worthy of full respect. (If anyone does not know how to manage his own family, how can he take care of God's church?) He must not be a recent convert, or he may become conceited and fall under the same judgment as the devil. He must also have a good reputation with outsiders, so that he will not fall into disgrace and into the devil's trap.

In the same way, deacons are to be worthy of respect, sincere, not indulging in much wine, and not pursuing dishonest gain. They must keep hold of the deep truths of the faith with a clear conscience. They must first be tested; and then if there is nothing against them, let them serve as deacons.

In the same way, the women are to be worthy of respect, not malicious talkers but temperate and trustworthy in everything.

A deacon must be faithful to his wife and must manage his children and his household well. Those who have served well gain an excellent standing and great assurance in their faith in Christ Jesus.

Ephesians 4:11-16:

So Christ himself gave the apostles, the prophets, the evangelists, the pastors and teachers, to equip his people for works of service, so that the body of Christ may be built up until we all reach unity in the faith and in the knowledge of the Son of God and become mature, attaining to the whole measure of the fullness of Christ.

Then we will no longer be infants, tossed back and forth by the waves, and blown here and there by every wind of teaching and by the cunning and craftiness of people in their deceitful scheming. Instead, speaking the truth in love, we will grow to become in every respect the mature body of Him Who is the head, that is, Christ. From Him the whole body, joined and held together by every supporting ligament, grows and builds itself up in love, as each part does its work.

Titus 1:7-9:

Since an overseer manages God's household, he must be blameless—not overbearing, not quick-tempered, not given to drunkenness, not violent, not pursuing dishonest gain. Rather, he must be hospitable, one who loves what is good, who is self-controlled, upright, holy and disciplined. He must hold firmly to the trustworthy message as it has been taught, so that he can encourage others by sound doctrine and refute those who oppose it.

1 Peter 5:1-5:

To the elders among you, I appeal as a fellow elder and a witness of Christ's sufferings who also will share in the glory to be revealed: Be shepherds of God's flock that is under your care, watching over them—not because you must, but because you are willing, as God wants you to be; not pursuing dishonest gain, but eager to serve; not lording it over those entrusted to you, but being examples to the flock. And when the Chief Shepherd appears, you will receive the crown of glory that will never fade away.

In the same way, you who are younger, submit yourselves to your elders. All of you, clothe yourselves with humility toward one another, because,

"God opposes the proud
  but shows favor to the humble."

It's very important we recognize service is a part of ministry work, especially when it comes to men. As a woman in ministry, I can testify to the severe gender gap present in most ministry circumstances. This manifests in the way that different genders are treated. I have seen one too many men who travel everywhere with an entourage, with women fawning all over them everywhere they go like groupies, requesting outlandish accommodations, wearing ridiculous outfits, and demanding outrageous amounts of money –

and getting all of it. If a woman does these things, she is accused of being Jezebel, of not being humble enough for ministry, or of somehow fleecing the flock. Women's offerings are also notoriously less than men's, because men are viewed as having to take care of their families (even when they are single and don't have a family). There is still an underlying message that any non-male individual is preaching by undeserved favor, whereas a male preaching is a favor extended to the congregation. These attitudes have created severe dissonant attitudes in the pulpit and in the way men present themselves versus the way others present themselves. I don't deny there are arrogant individuals of all genders out there who make ridiculous demands and act like pulpit prima donnas. There are far more men, however, who make their oyster and then act like they are its missing pearl.

Yes, the church should be of service to the minister who serves them, but that service is symbiotic, not only flowing in the minister's direction. Ministry is service, which means a lot of what is done in ministry requires the sacrifice of the minister involved. I don't personally know any ministers who don't have to work other jobs to keep their ministries afloat. Most aren't even doing that without struggling, even with a job. Ministry costs money, it costs time, and it costs the personal investment of the minister, made in each situation and with each person that comes up under a ministry. If you are in ministry to be served, you are missing the boat because ministry itself is here to serve.

If you are man called into ministry, you are called to hold down the following:

- **Handle household matters:** Being in ministry cannot come at the expense of everyone in your personal life. The first decision a man who is in ministry needs to make is discerning his call to be married or single. It is very possible that sometimes we are called to be or do something for a season, and discerning those seasons is the difference between success and balance or crashing and burning. If you want to have a family, you must remember you are called to serve your family as well as your ministry. How you balance that is up to you, but it is essential that you don't become an absentee husband, father, or minister in the process.

- **Responsible finances**: Ministry is about good stewardship, and good stewardship is about more than what we do with our gifts and our time. It's also about how well we handle what we have been given. You don't have to have a ton of money to run a good ministry, but you need to be faithful with the money you have.

- **Good character**: Yes, it is true there will always be someone who has something bad to say about a leader, especially in these times. People's expectations can be quite high and quite unrealistic. That having been said, ministers still should aspire for good character, and refrain from behaviors or attitudes that will give people the impression that ministry is something scornful.

- **Personal and ministerial accountability**: We have leaders in Christianity for a reason. If you are a leader, you need to make sure you have a leader as well who is able to train you in the level of training you need, listen to you when you need to talk, discipline you if it becomes necessary. and encourage you when you need encouragement.

<u>Living as servants</u>

At the end of the day, the Apostles Peter, Paul, and John had one powerful thing in common: they knew Christ made a difference in their lives, and they desired to be more like Him. It doesn't matter when they came to this realization; all that matters is they came to it, When they did, they changed within themselves what needed changing so they could move forward. As a man, have you made this same decision in your life? Is God in control of every aspect of your life, your call, your ministry? Do you seek His face when you come in or go out?

John 12:26:

Whoever serves Me must follow Me. Then My servant will be with Me everywhere I am. My Father will honor anyone who serves Me. (EXB)

Whether servanthood comes easily for you and helps you to find your place in this crazy world or whether it is something harder for you to develop, take another look at the men of the early church. Look at them as men, all of whom faced many of the same difficulties and challenges that you face, right now. They overcame them one at a time, and were still in the process of overcoming them, even as they served in ministry. They weren't perfect, but they were faithful, just as you are called to be. If you can master faithfulness, you can master servanthood, serving as a man set apart for God who knows that he's the most successful when he lays down his life for others.

Reflections

- Would you describe yourself as a type of Apostle John or more of an Apostle Peter/Paul type?

- How can you be a better example?

- When you look at the transformation of the Apostles Peter and Paul, what do you think about the process of transformation? How has God worked to transform you in your own life?

- How can we continue to serve in ways that will be current with our times?

- How can men who are ministers balance their

service in the best way possible?

10
Men Serving as Church Members

—————————x( )x—————————

When you come to the land which the Lord will give you, as He has promised, you shall keep this service.
(Exodus 12:25, AMPC)

- **Reading assignment:** The Books of Romans and Colossians

W e've spent the past several chapters looking at examples of men in the Bible either in ways we've never considered or with men we've never really looked at much, if at all. The next few chapters of this book will look at male service in specific capacities, of which we don't have one singular big-figure Bible male to point to as an example. Just because we don't have one man to point to doesn't mean we don't have relevant passages to back up what we will discuss, and it also doesn't mean what we are talking about is of lesser importance.

Here we will be looking at men serving as members of a church. This includes every male member of the church, and more specifically, men who are not in church service as pertains to ministry. If you're male and not in ministry, there's nothing wrong with you. Some men are called to ministry, and some are not, and there's nothing wrong with men who are not. It gets tricky because the majority of Bible men we tend to draw from were men who were in ministry, and that can give the impression that in order to be important or relevant, you have to be a minister. We may not look enough at men who didn't have a ministry call, but nothing is further from the truth. Whether you are in ministry or not, you are an important part of the church. Your participation in church is not just essential for you, but also for the church to get done what needs doing. If you are a Christian, you are a part of God's body, and what you have is needed. It doesn't matter if you are called to preach full-time or be a minister. What you have is just as important as what someone else has, and what you have to offer is what you need to offer.

I know from being a part of church (different denominations, of course) for most of my life that overall women do most of the "heavy lifting" at church. It is often the women who are behind most events, work most of the behind-the-scenes knowhow, and often get little to no acclaim or appreciation for what they do. This is not the way church is supposed to be. Women were not made for service while men are served. We're all believers, we are all made for service, and if you are a man who hasn't been doing your part in the Kingdom – now is the time to step up and get involved.

<u>Attending church</u>

In my chapter on Hosea, I tapped a little bit into how important it is for a man to have his own relationship with God, regardless of where the rest of their family is with their faith. We've made it generally acceptable for women to do this; in fact, it's often expected. Women are supposed to be the intercessors and churchgoers for their families, especially if the rest of the family does not attend. We don't tend to expect the same from men, however. If a man is a believer and his spouse or children are not following suit, we often expect the man to be quiet about his faith, not attend church, and not do anything to upset their domestic situation. It's also often unspoken that a man being faithful to

God will cause him marital problems, so he should refrain from church services or being very involved if his family is opposed or not involved in his faith.

I'm not sure why this strange double standard exists. It doesn't make sense, even in the context of our faith. We know the Bible educates on the ways to be good witnesses, It only stands to reason that for a man to display a good faith to his family involves his conduct, his continued dedication to the Lord, and his continued involvement with the church, despite the protests he might encounter from his family.

If you have a spouse or family interested in church, you have no excuse for not attending. If they are not attending, you need to find a church and attend anyway. If you have questions about going to a church, the best option is to visit, talk to the minister in charge, and find out more about what that particular church is all about. Different churches tend to have different themes or different outreaches, and if you want to make sure you are somewhere that will meet the needs you or you and your family will have, the best answer is to be upfront and find out.

1 Corinthians 3:7-16:

So neither he who plants is anything nor he who waters, but [only] God Who makes it grow and become greater. He who plants and he who waters are equal (one in aim, of the same importance and esteem), yet each shall receive his own reward (wages), according to his own labor. For we are fellow workmen (joint promoters, laborers together) with and for God; you are God's garden and vineyard and field under cultivation, [you are] God's building.

According to the grace (the special endowment for my task) of God bestowed on me, like a skillful architect and master builder I laid [the] foundation, and now another [man] is building upon it. But let each [man] be careful how he builds upon it. For no other foundation can anyone lay than that which is [already] laid, which is Jesus Christ (the Messiah, the Anointed One). But if anyone builds upon the Foundation, whether it be with gold, silver, precious stones, wood, hay, straw, The work of each [one] will become [plainly, openly] known (shown for what it is); for the day [of Christ] will disclose and declare it, because it will be revealed with fire, and the fire will test and critically appraise the character and worth of the work each person has done. If the work which any person has built on this Foundation [any product of his efforts whatever] survives [this test], he will get his reward. But if any person's work is burned up [under the test], he will suffer the loss [of it all, losing his reward], though he himself will be saved, but only as [one who has passed] through fire. Do you not discern and understand that you [the whole church at Corinth] are God's temple (His sanctuary), and that God's Spirit has His permanent dwelling in you [to be at home in you, collectively as a church and also individually]? (AMPC)

Hebrews 10:25:

You should not stay away from [neglect; forsake] the church meetings [meeting together], as some are doing [some were abandoning Christianity and returning to Judaism], but you should encourage each other [to stay faithful to Christ and to other believers], and even more so as you see the day coming [the day of the Lord, when Christ will return]. (EXB)

It's wrong to assume a man doesn't need church because he is a man. All human beings need social interaction with other human beings of like beliefs. We all need community! It's also wrong to assume that being in a family means you don't need social and spiritual interaction outside of that family unit. Even the best and strongest of families need good spiritual leadership, good friends and prayer partners, and social networks of individuals who are also believers. Spiritual connection through church helps us to build up our faith, learn how to interact with other individuals, to share ideas, accept differences, and learn more about what is truly important as we pursue spiritual ground.

Any survey of churches the world over will show a large percentage of female participation with a minority of male participation. The only men you might see are in leadership: those who are ministers or in some other sort of ministry leadership, such as deacons or elders. Such men usually take roles pertaining to financial distribution, ushers, distribution of communion or taking the collection (this is if such a position is different from an usher). Even in recent years, I am seeing fewer men in these positions as they are often delegated to women who are identified as "greeters" or to children or teenagers. A quick glance around a church finds more women than men and the few men who are in attendance often less than enthusiastic about participation.

We've taught men overall that their attendance and presence is enough. We don't encourage them to try to be involved, especially if something doesn't interest them. There has been enough propaganda against men's involvement with church over the past 25 years to give men the distinct impression they don't have to be involved, and if they show up, they are doing more than their share.

We need to break through this mentality. It is hurting men (and the church at large) in more than one way. Life isn't all about what happens or who shows up at church. The concept of showing up as enough, without the man really getting involved or participating in things can negatively impact a marriage, parenthood, home life, dating or intimate relationships, work, and life in general. Men need to know that being interpersonal takes work, and being in relationships requires effort. It's not as simple as deciding to show up and hope that's enough.

Romans 12:1-2:

Therefore, I urge you, brothers and sisters, in view of God's mercy, to offer your bodies as a living sacrifice, holy and pleasing to God—this is your true and proper worship. Do not conform to the pattern of this world, but be transformed by the renewing of your mind. Then you will be able to test and approve what God's will is—his good, pleasing and perfect will.

Servants don't just show up; they serve. They are actively involved with household or professional matters to make sure those they serve are comfortable, their needs are met, and all duties and responsibilities are completed. They are participants in what they do and eager to be seen as competent and responsible. The same should be true for every Christian. Being part of the church is about more than just showing up on occasion or even every week. It's about setting your mind to the following:

- You are a Christian
- You are a part of the body of Christ, and you are a part of the church
- You attend this church to serve, not to be served
- You are going to find opportunities to be involved in church
- You are going to keep this commitment because it is part of your relationship with God

Being involved

There are many people who aren't involved in church because they aren't sure where to start with involvement. I'm not a leader who beats around the bush when it comes to needing help, but I do know there are ministers out there who don't readily admit they need assistance in church activities. Even in churches that do make their needs known, it is sometimes unclear who to talk to or what one must do in order to function in that ministry.

1 Peter 4:10-11:

Each of you should use whatever gift you have received to serve others, as faithful stewards of God's grace in its various forms. If anyone speaks, they should do so as one who speaks the very words of God. If anyone serves, they should do so with the strength God provides, so that in all things

God may be praised through Jesus Christ. To Him be the glory and the power for ever and ever. Amen.

If your church isn't making known where they need help right now, the best thing to do is ask about what help is needed and where. Ask people who function in different ministries or go directly to your spiritual leader and ask for a list or for different areas where you can be of service to be more involved.

Ministry helps

Most church operations function via the world of helps ministries, or those works that relate to helping the church to operate. "Helps" are a general area of spiritual gifts that are specifically about service. They are under a category of governance known as the "works of the church" which are overseen by the appointment ministries of bishops, elders, and deacons as well as those who operate in the Ephesians 4:11 ministry. In order to be a part of helps ministry work, it is very important that you keep your focus on the following:

- **Training:** Some churches require general training for all helps ministry participants. Some require further training in order to function in specific helps work. If you are going to do it, instead of grumbling over training, make a point to do your training with excellence.

- **Commitment:** The work of helps can't function if people say they will be there and then don't show up. Make sure that whatever you say you are going to do is exactly what you do, even if it is inconvenient when the time comes.

- **Punctuality:** When it's your turn to serve, be on time, not several minutes late. If you can't be somewhere due to an emergency, call as soon as you know you won't be able to make it.

- **Purpose:** There are no small or insignificant tasks in helps. Everything that needs to be done is important and relevant to the survival of the church and to its growth and function on a regular basis.

In most churches, there are two forms of helps ministry: primary helps and secondary helps. Primary helps relate to works of the church that are regularly needed for church function. These require the participation of all possible servants, as they are regularly needed. Primary helps are directly connected to weekly services and ministry functions within the church body itself. Secondary helps are works that aren't required as frequently, but most likely relate to outreaches or other works that are done from time to time and do need servants to help and participate. These often include community outreaches and general works that benefit the community. It is my recommendation that everyone in a church find at least one primary helps work and one secondary helps work to be fully involved and engaged in church activities.

Primary helps:
- Leadership assistance (armor bearers, assistants, adjutants, etc.)
- Altar work
- Announcements
- Office/business work
- Ushers/greeters
- Praise and worship team/choir
- Audio/visual ministry
- Social media assistance
- Children's ministry (children's church, nursery, Sunday school, Vacation Bible School)
- Youth ministry
- Women's and men's ministries
- Building maintenance

Secondary helps:
- Arts/dance ministry

- Hospitality
- Homeless outreach
- Widows/orphans
- Clothing drives
- Street evangelism
- Food banks
- Shelter ministries
- Drug/alcohol ministry
- Community counseling
- Community projects

The church you are in might have all these outreaches, they might have some of them, or they might have different ones. No matter what list of helps your church specifically has, make a point to serve in both a regular ministry that serves the church and another one that has an outreach quality to it, reaching far beyond the immediate walls of the church.

Proverbs 11:25:

A generous person will prosper;
whoever refreshes others will be refreshed.

Proverbs 19:17:

Whoever is kind to the poor lends to the Lord,
and He will reward them for what they have done.

Matthew 5:16:

In the same way, let your light shine before others, that they may see your good deeds and glorify your Father in heaven.

Luke 6:38:

Give, and it will be given to you. A good measure, pressed down, shaken together and running over, will be poured into your lap. For with the measure you use, it will be measured to you.

These different service opportunities remind us that being a part of church is more than just about going and sitting in a pew. True servanthood is about serving in church and serving the community, too.

Spiritual gifts

I can't rightly encourage you to service and not talk about spiritual gifts, at least in some educational sense. I know many preachers talk about spiritual gifts or encourage people to use theirs, but they don't talk about what they are or how to discern or distinguish them in one's life. This has caused a lot of people to think certain gifts are more important or desirable than others and left too many people assuming they must have the most important gifts so they can be the most important people. This sort of idea is causing terrible strife in the church, as spiritual gifts are used to generate attention and personal fanfare rather than spiritual edification and purpose.

In this chapter, we are looking at the charisma gifts, or those spiritual gifts open to anyone in the Body of Christ, at any time. They are found in 1 Corinthians 12:4-11 and 28 and Romans 12:3-8.

There are different kinds of gifts, but the same Spirit distributes them. There are different kinds of service, but the same Lord. There are different kinds of working, but in all of them and in everyone it is the same God at work.

Now to each one the manifestation of the Spirit is given for the common good. To one there is given through the Spirit a message of wisdom, to another a message of knowledge by means of the same Spirit, to another faith by the same Spirit, to another gifts of healing by that one Spirit, to another miraculous powers, to another prophecy, to another distinguishing between spirits, to another speaking in different kinds of tongues, and to still another the interpretation of tongues. All these are the work of one and the same Spirit, and He distributes them to each one, just as He determines...And God has placed in the church first of all apostles, second prophets, third teachers, then miracles, then gifts of healing, of helping, of guidance, and of different kinds of tongues.

For by the grace given me I say to every one of you: Do not think of yourself more highly than you ought, but rather think of yourself with sober judgment, in accordance with the faith God has distributed to each of you. For just as each of us has one body with many members, and these members do not all have the same function, so in Christ we, though many, form one body, and each member belongs to all the others. We have different gifts, according to the grace given to each of us. If your gift is prophesying, then prophesy in accordance with your faith; if it is serving, then serve; if it is teaching, then teach; if it is to encourage, then give encouragement; if it is giving, then give generously; if it is to lead, do it diligently; if it is to show mercy, do it cheerfully.

In my book, *Ministry School Boot Camp: Training For Helps Ministries, Appointments, And Beyond* (Righteous Pen Publications, 2012), I explain the different spiritual gifts as follows:

- **Word of Wisdom:** A word of wisdom is the ability to give insight, relevance, and revelation into a situation that one knows nothing about. It is a form of prophecy, but differs in that a word of wisdom almost always requires the obedience and action of the receiver of the *logos* (revelation, essence) or *rhema* (spoken word) revelation. This means a word of wisdom is conditional; its effects and purposes will not be made productive without the acceptance and action of the receiver.

- **Word of Knowledge:** A word of knowledge is the ability to give applicable knowledge and advice about a situation that you know nothing about, or a word of insight into something that speaks to the receiver. It too, like a word of wisdom, is a form of prophecy, but differs in that a word of knowledge may or may not require the obedience and action of the receiver. A word of knowledge may just prove God to an individual (making a proclamation about someone's job, circumstance, or age, for example), may call something out (such as an illness, a hidden sin, or a calling that has remained under wraps) or may also offer someone's knowledgeable solutions and advice for a particular situation.

- **Faith:** We know that, as believers, we are called to have faith, it being the substance (or stuff) of things hoped for, the evidence (or proof) of things not seen. Faith is, therefore, a spiritual gift every believer should have. I believe in the context it is spoken of here, however, we are able to imply there are different levels of faith and different proportions of faith given to each believer. When someone has the gift of faith they have faith as an enduring gift, trust, and focus on God that supersedes everything else in their lives. Individuals with a gift of faith know how to keep the church focused on God, in every season.

- **Healing:** It's easy to assume healing is only about people getting out of wheelchairs, but the truth of healing is that there are many ways in which we, as people, require healing. To have a gift of healing means an individual operates in the power of God to bring about His needed touch, whether physical, emotional, mental, or spiritual. Most obviously, this is done via the laying on of hands and prayer, but there are those who are able to bring about healing and comfort through prayer, counseling, and assistance, as well.

- **Miracles:** A miracle is a supernatural occurrence with no explanation in the natural realm. They are things that happen and cannot be explained by science. Miracles vary from supernatural occurrences that relate to magic or the occult because they happen without the different cyclical workings in order to bring their methods to fruition (witchcraft). Miracles are done by God, and God alone, and serve His incredible purposes. A miracle event would be someone unable to walk from birth suddenly being able to do so due to the spiritual intercession of a minister of God.

- **Prophecy:** Prophecy is a big subject. It is also probably one of the most misunderstood subjects in relation to the believer today. The major reason it is misunderstood? Many people assume having a prophetic gift makes one a "prophet." This is incorrect. The gift of prophecy can extend to anyone in the church – God can give someone a prophetic revelation or insight into a situation at any time – if they are in the Spirit of God. Rather than being a full-time calling, prophecy moves within an individual with a prophetic gift at God's operation, as it is needed. It is also confused because there is more than one way in which a prophetic gift may manifest. Prophecy is not speaking cars, houses, and money over people. It's not telling you the date you'll meet your future spouse, or acting as a misguided horoscope at the end of an offering line. True prophecy manifests as an individual moves in an area of seeing or foretelling an event, has a dream or encounter with God that reveals something important about the future, works in writing, music, dance or other arts, or works in prophecy and prophetic interpretation. The prophetic speaks for God, making His will known to humanity. This flows within the prophetic realm, God's presence of eternity (*karios* time), as the individual exercising prophecy conveys His message to His people.

- **Discernment of Spirits:** The gift of discerning spirits is an intense experience, knowing what is God from what is not God. Just because something seems to be favorable or un-favorable is not a simple enough explanation to know whether or not that thing – be it a spirit or spiritual operation – is of God. The spiritual realm is not simple enough to polarize into "like" and "dislike" or the random ways we judge people by what we see or perceive in the flesh. Sometimes God moves in our lives to remove things, and sometimes He moves to give things. Something that can sound great and wonderful can be out of God's will for us, and something that sounds awful can easily be exactly where we need to be for a time. Discernment of spirits is the operation of this sorting it all out – whether or not something is God or not, and whether or not something should be pursued, entertained, or accepted.

- **Diverse Tongues:** Also called the "baptism of the Holy Spirit" in some groups. We often call this "speaking in tongues," by which an individual speaks in a prayer language of heaven rather than an earthly language. Studies have proven that when speaking in tongues, the believer's language center shuts down and the spiritual center of the brain is exclusively active, thus making it a real and viable phenomenon. This is probably one of the most common gifts experienced by believers in the church today. It is also one of the most counterfeited. Tongues is a genuine language, though not one of this earth. Sounds made (such as na, na, na or da, da, da) that mimic earthly tones or words do not classify as tongues. Tongues can serve as a personal prayer language engaging the intercession of the Spirit, or as a word for the entire body of believers.

- **Interpretation of Tongues:** If a word is given in tongues for a group of believers, that word must be interpreted. It doesn't make sense for someone to stand up in front of a congregation and prattle on and on in a language people present cannot understand. Interpretation, therefore, is essential, that the word delivered in tongues may be understood by all present.

- **Ministry:** The word "ministry" literally means "service." The gift of ministry is also sometimes called the gift of hospitality or service, because its work can encompass these different things that help people to feel comfortable and encouraged by meeting necessary needs. I think it's interesting that ministry service is noted as being a gift available to all in the church, especially in a time when it is generally believed a ministry to be the responsibility of and belong exclusively to a singular leader. If "ministry" is a charismatic gift, that means people are called to serve within a ministry, whether or not they are themselves called to full-time ministry work. The Bible does not tell us specifically how to be of service, indicating any gift offered for the work of ministry is appropriate ministry service. Anyone who has a gift to be offered should, therefore, operate a gift of ministry service.

- **Helps:** Helps, also called the ministry of helps and also a part of the works of the church, is the focus of this particular book. Helps is a broad category of church service used to describe any and all aspects of a church or ministry that relate to the regular operations of an organization. They are called "helps" because they assist the formal ministers of a congregation with areas of church ministry that are

231

too numerous for them to directly run, operate, and function themselves, and also because they are a general "help," or service, to the Christian community where they function, as a whole.

- **Administration/Government:** The term for "administration" in the Greek literally means "to stand out front." This indicates accountability in action. An administrator has the desire and willingness to step up and lead, the while implementing the instructions handed down to accomplish this goal. Administration, also called governance, is leadership or the ability to lead, with one major difference. In a gift of administration, one is not just a leader, but also an organizer, an implementer of structure and efficiency. Through a gift of administration, the church is able to stand with details of implementation and order properly answered. Administrators help to continue the structure implemented in every church by an apostle.

- **Teaching:** Like prophecy, the gift of teaching is different from the office of a teacher, with the same major distinction: one who teaches as an office does it constantly and consistently, while one with a gift of teaching does it as the opportunity may arise. A gift of teaching means one has the ability to instruct others, and this may come about for any age group or audience, and in many forms (including public instruction, private instruction, media ministry, or writing).

- **Exhortation:** Exhortation is a fancy word that means "to edify" or "build up." In the context of faith, one who exhorts builds up and edifies one's relationship with God and all that goes along with it. It does not merely mean "to encourage," because one can encourage someone into incorrect territory. One who exhorts has the ability to break things down into individual steps, make them more understandable, and make the way of God clear in an understandable context. Through God's means to the individual, one who exhorts may speak, pray, counsel, or equip individuals to do exactly what God has for them to do.

- **Leadership:** We've already established not every person in the church is called to Ephesians 4:11 ministry leadership. A further confirmation is the gift of "leadership," or "leading," by which someone is a leader in some capacity, but is not in Ephesians 4:11 ministry leadership. This particular gift is essential for those in the appointment works of elder, bishop, and deacon, because these roles serve a leadership function. It may also apply to someone who assists in a team effort or work, or leads a Bible study or home ministry, who is not in the Ephesians 4:11 ministry.

- **Giving:** Much like the gift of faith, there are some people endowed with a heart and mind to give. Instead of giving out of mere obligation, giving is a spiritual purpose in their lives. They are eager to contribute to God's work however they can, giving of whatever they have, and are excited to do so. Someone with a gift of giving will budget their money, set aside special time, and make whatever is theirs available for the Kingdom, freely, without having to be consistently asked, without having to twist their arms, and happy to multiply their resources to continue to give for the Kingdom of God. Givers can be found in any capacity in a ministry, and will serve as a blessing to both the leader and congregation with their giving.

- **Mercy:** A "mercy gift," as it is often called, is a desire to see an end to suffering. Individuals with this gift are quick to recognize when someone is having a problem or a difficult time, recognizing when something is off or going awry. The gift of mercy sees someone through issues with love and empathy, and recognizes the value in those who might be difficult to love. Some Bible translations define the gift of mercy as "giving," because mercy is, indeed, a true gift.

Talents and abilities

As human beings, we don't just have spiritual gifts. We also have natural talents and abilities. We often refer to these things as "gifts," which can become confusing when we start talking about spiritual gifts in addition to these things we have by nature. I don't refer to them as gifts, but rather talents and abilities, to make a distinction between the two in our understanding. While the talents and abilities that we have are there by God's grace and gifting, they aren't spiritual gifts.

Exodus 31:3-5:

and I have filled him with the Spirit of God, with wisdom, with understanding, with knowledge and with all kinds of skills— to make artistic designs for work in gold, silver and bronze, to cut and set stones, to work in wood, and to engage in all kinds of crafts.

Exodus 35:10:

All who are skilled among you are to come and make everything the Lord has commanded.

Psalm 150:3-6:

Praise Him with the sounding of the trumpet,
praise Him with the harp and lyre,
praise Him with timbrel and dancing,
praise Him with the strings and pipe,
praise Him with the clash of cymbals,
praise Him with resounding cymbals.

Let everything that has breath praise the Lord.

Praise the Lord.

Example of talents and abilities are:

- Playing a musical instrument
- Having an aptitude for a subject, such as science or math
- Memorization
- Networking
- Self-management
- Marketing
- Photography
- Sense of humor
- Management of others
- Positive visualization
- Communicating with others
- Juggling
- Athleticism
- Financial management
- Life maintenance
- Computer skills

Having these things are for our general benefit in life, giving us the ability to not only enjoy life, but to be good at and excel at things. They help us to be able to work, to function and, when it comes to God's Kingdom, to serve. Just as our spiritual gifts are for God's glory, so too are our natural talents and abilities. When looking at our lives, our first question should always be, "What can I do with what I have to better the Kingdom of God by blessing someone else's life?" The more we do for others, the happier we will be as people, and the more we will experience God's blessing.

<u>Using what we have for God's service</u>

1 Corinthians 12:12-27 reveals to us much about why God gives to us so graciously as people in our spiritual gifts,

talents, and abilities:

Just as a body, though one, has many parts, but all its many parts form one body, so it is with Christ. For we were all baptized by one Spirit so as to form one body—whether Jews or Gentiles, slave or free—and we were all given the one Spirit to drink. Even so the body is not made up of one part but of many.

Now if the foot should say, "Because I am not a hand, I do not belong to the body," it would not for that reason stop being part of the body. And if the ear should say, "Because I am not an eye, I do not belong to the body," it would not for that reason stop being part of the body. If the whole body were an eye, where would the sense of hearing be? If the whole body were an ear, where would the sense of smell be? But in fact God has placed the parts in the body, every one of them, just as He wanted them to be. If they were all one part, where would the body be? As it is, there are many parts, but one body.

The eye cannot say to the hand, "I don't need you!" And the head cannot say to the feet, "I don't need you!" On the contrary, those parts of the body that seem to be weaker are indispensable, and the parts that we think are less honorable we treat with special honor. And the parts that are unpresentable are treated with special modesty, while our presentable parts need no special treatment. But God has put the body together, giving greater honor to the parts that lacked it, so that there should be no division in the body, but that its parts should have equal concern for each other. If one part suffers, every part suffers with it; if one part is honored, every part rejoices with it.

Now you are the body of Christ, and each one of you is a part of it.

The reason God has given to us so abundantly through spiritual gifts, talents, and abilities is so we can do His work in this world. We gain proper understanding of such (or we should, ideally) as we attend church, and we grow in our knowledge of the Scriptures. As we study, we gain a deeper understanding of ourselves and where we fit in God's bigger Kingdom picture. All of us – even you, reading this book – has a purpose to fulfil here in the Kingdom. What you have to offer is just as valuable and important as the next person, and God has given you your unique combination of spiritual gifts, talents, and abilities to offer yourself as a servant for Him, making a difference in the lives of other people.

Reflections

- How do you feel about church and going to church?

- How can you be more involved in your church life?

- What are some of your spiritual gifts?

- What are some of your natural talents and abilities?

- How can you use what you have to be of service to others?

11
MEN SERVING AS THE SPOUSE
OF A MINISTER

———————————•( )•———————————

IF ANYONE FAILS TO PROVIDE FOR HIS RELATIVES, AND ESPECIALLY FOR THOSE OF HIS OWN
FAMILY, HE HAS DISOWNED THE FAITH [BY FAILING TO ACCOMPANY IT WITH FRUITS]
AND IS WORSE THAN AN UNBELIEVER [WHO PERFORMS HIS OBLIGATION IN THESE MATTERS].
(1 TIMOTHY 5:8, AMPC)

- **Reading assignment:** Judges 4:4-5 and the Book of
Proverbs

Over the past decade, I have received many questions from women in special circumstances about the role their husbands should play in their lives. Their special circumstance? The women are called to ministry, but their husbands are not. They have heard the various theories about husbands and wives, men and women, and the general confusion that tends to ensue when the topic comes up in a ministry setting. They are confused because nobody teaches the same thing or reads the Scriptures in quite the same way, thus they don't really know how to respond with the rise of women in ministry and husbands who prefer to sit on the sidelines or serve in church in a different way.

Trying to follow everyone's advice is confusing. When it doesn't work, they step back and start all over again. When they don't understand what direction to take and are under pressure from all sorts of sources to conform their relationship to someone else's expectations, they find themselves at odds and strained because the world has entered their relationship.

As of the edit on this book, I've been married twice. In both marriages, neither my late husband served, nor my current husband serves in ministry. Despite the unique challenges I've had in both situations, ministry is my call, not theirs. My husband's assignment is to build our business and take care of me, making sure I can focus on this call, rather than worrying about things such as bills, paying the mortgage, and my personal safety and security. We have different purposes, but it gets the job done.

When a spouse is in ministry and their husband is not, the two of them need to figure out what works best for them in terms of their own balancing act between home, family, and ministry. It's vital that the two accept one another, just as they are, with the unique gifts and callings they both have in their lives. It's not a perfect balance, or always a successful one, but it is one that merits examination, especially in the day and age in which we live. The only way such a relationship can be successful is if the man has a proper understanding of service and a solid understanding of who he is as a man and that this is exactly where God has called him to be.

Cutting out the confusion

Awhile back, someone added me on Facebook. Harmless enough, right? The discussion went downhill from there. He tried to speak with me in a manner that was both confusing and disheartening to me as both a woman and a minister. This was someone I didn't know, had no interest in personally (or professionally, for that matter). He immediately told me he believed the man was the "head" of the woman and he could see how that would cause problems in our correspondence. When I tried to point out it was rather ridiculous to come at me in such a manner both offensive and incorrect, he accused me of being irrational and overreacting. He didn't seem to understand that no matter what his views were, he was attempting to subordinate me to himself. Such was not only offensive, it was out of true order and was also unnecessary.

There is still very much a glass ceiling for women who desire to proclaim the Gospel. We hear all the time that "all things are possible," but if you spend any time in the faith at all these days, there is an asterisk next to the verse in many preachers' notes and minister's guidebooks. Some say a woman can never teach or preach. As much as I'd like to tell you that's a rare viewpoint today, there are more out there with this belief system than we might like to admit. There are others who believe if a woman is in ministry her husband must be in it and fill a subordinate position along with him. By extension, if she ministers, she must do so with his permission. Some feel he must always be present with her. Others feel if a woman is to be in ministry, she is still subordinate to a man at home. That means she must "turn off" her ministry/authority side the second she enters the door and yield herself to her husband. It's easy to see where these belief spill over. If he is boss at home, there are going to be times when ministry overflows into the home. If he is not on board with that, there will be conflict.

Does anyone else see the amount of hypothetically created not-having-to-exist conflict in all of this? I don't recall any Bible verses that state a woman can't be in ministry or that there should be all these conflicting rules presenting power and control into a marital relationship because a woman is in ministry. Whenever a marital partner decides to do something major, it has the potential for complications at home. Yet I don't ever hear any discussion about the impact of absentee ministry fathers on their spouses or children. Nobody ever stands up and calls out men who neglect their families due to ministry. No one ever says their attitudes are disrespectful or unfair to their spouses or families.

2 Kings 22:14:

Hilkiah the priest, Ahikam, Akbor, Shaphan and Asaiah went to speak to the prophet Huldah, who was the wife of Shallum son of Tikvah, the son of Harhas, keeper of the wardrobe. She lived in Jerusalem, in the New Quarter.

2 Chronicles 34:22:

Hilkiah and those the king had sent with him went to speak to the prophet Huldah, who was the wife of Shallum son of Tokhath, the son of Hasrah, keeper of the wardrobe. She lived in Jerusalem, in the New Quarter.

Acts 18:26:

He began to speak boldly in the synagogue. When Priscilla and Aquila heard him, they invited him to their home and explained to him the way of God more adequately.

Romans 16:3:

Greet Priscilla and Aquila, my co-workers in Christ Jesus.

Romans 16:7: .

Greet Andronicus and Junia, my fellow Jews who have been in prison with me. They are outstanding among the apostles, and they were in Christ before I was.

1 Corinthians 9:5:

Don't we have the right to take a believing wife along with us, as do the other apostles and the Lord's brothers and Cephas?

There are Biblical examples where people worked as couples, as a team, or where someone worked by themselves. There is even evidence in at least one of these verses that the woman (Priscilla) held the superior ministerial position over the man (Aquila), because she is named first. I don't know, however, if they thought about their relationships in this way. Cultural subordination is on everyone's mind these days, particularly the idea of "who is in charge" at all times. This makes it more difficult to break through these concepts to see the truth about them. More than anything, we need to embrace the idea that God's intention for relationships across the gender spectrum was not to dominate and subordinate. Relationships built on love should reflect love in them, not power and control struggles.

Let's cut out the rules people have made for such a relationship and focus on the two people in that relationship. Yes, having a spouse in ministry is a challenge, regardless of their gender. It's especially difficult when the man isn't the one who is called. It has unique cultural challenges and differences, and those differences require a strong couple. Figuring out what works best for you, what works best with the calls you both have, and what will be best for you both and your family is what is most important. A man should never think he has the right to stand in the way of what God has called his spouse to do. Remember, God is still God. He is greater than you and He knows better than you do. You also should never feel pressured to take on an office or feel inadequate because your spouse is a minister. There is no reason why what they do has to change your whole life, just like what you do shouldn't change theirs. The two of you are coming together, working together, and producing a life, each one doing what they are supposed to do in Him.

Let me add here: if you are both called to ministry, if you are called to minister together or separately, and if you are called to different offices, that's all fine and good, too. It doesn't matter who is called to what or who is called to do what, because it's all about service. The point I am trying to make here is that there isn't a wrong way to have a marriage or a marriage where one or both spouses are in ministry. Just because it isn't following the rulebook of some man-made tradition doesn't mean you aren't married, and it doesn't mean you don't have a good marriage. Whatever circumstance you have within your marriage and the unique gifts you both have are exactly what God knows will benefit both of you. These provide you both a unique opportunity to serve. Don't let anyone pressure you into anything else, because the result will be a strain on your relationship.

Not all men are leaders

Let's get it an important generalization out of the way right now: not all men are leaders, just like not everyone else is a leader. Not all men are called to the highest positions of leadership either, just because they are men. Men are not called to leadership simply because they are men. If we can wrap our heads around that, it will make the remainder of understanding as pertains to this topic much, much easier. I've known many men who tried to aspire for higher leadership or leadership, period in life, only to find themselves frustrated, stressed, out of sorts, and unhappy. The second they gave up those aspirations for something else, they found peace. The universal answer they give for pursuing things for so many years is often summed up in one phrase: someone in their lives told them they needed to be on top of it all, so they pursued it, even though it made them miserable.

When I was in Europe about ten years ago, I was very taken aback to see the relationships between the men and the women. I heard a testimony of a couple where the man was more comfortable cooking and helping to keep the house up, and the woman was the frontrunner for the ministry. People always told them he had to be the minister, not her, because that wasn't the way things were done. They shared how difficult it was for them to overcome the stereotypes and concepts people had to function most effectively in the ministry they believed they were called to have. It was surprising to me how traditional they were expected to be in the church, especially given the women in Europe were liberated almost to the point of being domineering. These attitudes that men are supposed to be natural leaders, always be superior or greater to others, or are supposed to always have higher positions than everyone else, clearly transcend cultures. The expectations don't consider if anyone is comfortable with what they are forced to adapt to in their lives.

The Bible is quite clear that not all people are called to leadership. Even though we live in a world that kind of skirts around this fact, it remains true, nonetheless. Not everyone is given the grace to be a leader, and this includes men along with everyone else. Some people are perfectly content to live their lives simply and in peace, recognizing God has given them the ability to be where they are, and they accept that.

Matthew 22:14:

"For many are invited, but few are chosen."

Acts 15:22:

Then the apostles and elders, with the whole church, decided to choose some of their own men and send them to Antioch with Paul and Barnabas. They chose Judas (called Barsabbas) and Silas, men who were leaders among the believers.

Acts 20:28:

Keep watch over yourselves and all the flock of which the Holy Spirit has made you overseers. Be shepherds of the church of God, which He bought with His own blood.

Colossians 3:17:

And whatever you do, whether in word or deed, do it all in the name of the Lord Jesus, giving thanks to God the Father through Him.

Hebrews 13:17:

Have confidence in your leaders and submit to their authority, because they keep watch over you as those who must give an account. Do this so that their work will be a joy, not a burden, for that would be of no benefit to you.

James 3:1:

Not many of you should become teachers, my fellow believers, because you know that we who teach will be judged more strictly.

The same is true when it comes to a ministry call. Everyone is not called to serve in full-time or even part-time ministry, whether married or not, regardless of gender. It is perfectly possible for one partner to be called to ministry and their husband not called to ministry. People can live in harmony when one is a leader and one is not, quite well, and it doesn't matter who is the leader and who is not. What does matter is that if a man is not called to be in ministry or be a leader, that he is honest about that and accepts God's will for who he is rather than trying to change himself. It's also important that the couple accept and love one another for who they are, and recognize their service is different, thus making it purposeful.

Different service

God gives each one of us different gifts, abilities, and talents, as we discussed in the last chapter. This should be our first hint that nobody is a carbon copy of anyone else. We are all individually stamped with God's uniqueness, and that uniqueness is what gives us the ability to serve in the special way He appoints us to do so. We should never feel the pressure to be someone other than who we are or serve in a way that is contrary to our abilities.
1 Corinthians 12:1-7:

Now concerning spiritual gifts, brethren, I would not have you ignorant. Ye know that ye were Gentiles, carried away unto these dumb idols, even as ye were led. Wherefore I give you to understand, that no man speaking by the Spirit of God calleth Jesus accursed: and that no man can say that Jesus is the Lord, but by the Holy Ghost.

Now there are diversities of gifts, but the same Spirit. And there are differences of administrations, but the same Lord. And there are diversities of operations, but it is the same God which worketh all in all. But the manifestation of the Spirit is given to every man to profit withal. (KJV)

Your service, as a man, doesn't have to be the same as someone else's. Your spouse's service toward you doesn't have to be the same as someone else's. It doesn't have to follow the form of a cookie-cutter rule book. The way you serve, the priorities you have, and the way in which you interact doesn't have to be like everyone else's. It's all right to be different. And above all, it's all right for you, as a man, to serve your spouse.

Being Deborah's husband

In 2011, I started notes for a message called, "Being Deborah's Husband." I got the idea after talking to a friend of mine who was a minister and was having some problems in his marriage because the relationship the two of them had was not what we would classify as a "normal" situation. It was different because of his strong ministry call and the way it transformed his entire household. It was after meeting my friend that I started thinking about ministry and just how difficult it must be to be the "not-called-to-ministry" person in a relationship. We are always quick to talk about what a hard job it is for the minister, and it's true; it is a hard job. It almost feels impossible at times, and it definitely feels like someone always thinks we're doing it the wrong way or with the wrong vision. We encounter power and control, disrespectful treatment, and the feeling you can't move forward like you should. But it is equally difficult for the spouse who is not called into ministry (and even for some who are).

My first marriage was a complicated mire of confusion, frustration, and abuse. I spent most of it feeling like not only was I fighting for my ministry, I was also fighting my husband.

It wasn't until after he died that I could clearly see he didn't get the best part of having a wife in ministry, either. He watched others mistreat and disrespect me. He knew I wasn't receiving what I should have in offerings. He saw the struggle. Instead of developing empathy, he turned it on me. That part of the story isn't what we would consider to be "normal" among a marital couple, but it did make me think about things. Maybe if he saw a better side of ministry, he wouldn't have been so resistant to help me in it.

It's difficult to be the other spouse. They have to sit back and watch the way we're treated. They are called to support us in a work that doesn't always have use for us. They deal with the challenge of maintaining a relationship with a spouse who has an outstanding commitment – one to the Lord – which sometimes overflows, intrudes, or affects their marriage. It takes a lot to keep up balance, strength, and purpose as the one who is more in the background.

Judges 4:4-14:

And Deborah, a prophetess, the wife of Lapidoth, she judged Israel at that time. And she dwelt under the palm tree of Deborah between Ramah and Bethel in mount Ephraim: and the children of Israel came up to her for judgment. And she sent and called Barak the son of Abinoam out of Kedeshnaphtali, and said unto him, Hath not the LORD God of Israel commanded, saying, Go and draw toward mount Tabor, and take with thee ten thousand men of the children of Naphtali and of the children of Zebulun? And I will draw unto thee to the river Kishon Sisera, the captain of Jabin's army, with his chariots and his multitude; and I will deliver him into thine hand.

And Barak said unto her, If thou wilt go with me, then I will go: but if thou wilt not go with me, then I will not go. And she said, I will surely go with thee: notwithstanding the journey that thou takest shall not be for thine honour; for the LORD shall sell Sisera into the hand of a woman. And Deborah arose, and went with Barak to Kedesh. And Barak called Zebulun and Naphtali to Kedesh; and he went up with ten thousand men at his feet: and Deborah went up with him.

Now Heber the Kenite, which was of the children of Hobab the father in law of Moses, had severed himself from the Kenites, and pitched his tent unto the plain of Zaanaim, which is by Kedesh. And they shewed Sisera that Barak the son of Abinoam was gone up to mount Tabor. And Sisera gathered together all his chariots, even nine hundred chariots of iron, and all the people that were with him, from Harosheth of the Gentiles unto the river of Kishon. And Deborah said unto Barak, Up; for this is the day in which the LORD *hath delivered Sisera into thine hand: is not the* LORD *gone out before thee? So Barak went down from mount Tabor, and ten thousand men after him.* (KJV)

Deborah was not just the spiritual leader of Israel. She was also the military leader and a judge. She spent her days handling disputes, battle strategies, and what was in the best interest of the nation. It was almost like she was president and prophet at the same time, holding down an entire nation of people. That meant her husband, Lappidoth, had to accept the fact that she was a busy woman. She had a position that demanded he was of service to her so she could do exactly what she was created for – and supposed – to do.

This means: Lappidoth cooked dinner sometimes. He helped around the house. He helped out with care of various relatives. If she came home and was tired, he didn't hesitate to take her out to dinner or bring her a nice meal and help her be comfortable. He was considerate of her needs, he was attentive to her, and for what she needed, he was there for her. He knew the value of serving his wife. That helped them to have a long and successful relationship.

Whether you have a spouse in ministry, what I am about to say applies to you. In fact, they are in ministry, it applies in a bigger way, but it still applies either way. If you want to be successful in your marriage, you need to learn how to serve your spouse. Men need to serve in their marital relationships.

In a world where your spouse is not only a pioneer but also a trailblazer, it is that much more important for them to see that you love and believe in them. You show this through service: helping, not complaining, showing proper respect, doing what needs to be done, and comforting and providing what you can to make that much of a difference in their life.

In praise of your spouse

I don't know when we started treating Proverbs 31 like a big, long, impossible-to-reach to-do list in church, but when we approach it like this, it proves we don't have the first clue about it. Proverbs 31 is one of a handful of Bible passages frequently used against women, especially women in ministry. People think women should be x, y, and z in the same way as the woman in the passage, and if they are anything less, they aren't as godly as they can or should be.

This is the opposite of what Proverbs 31 is about. The evidence of this can be seen in Jewish culture. Proverbs 31 has always been used in praise of women for the many things they do, and for the way they do them well.

Proverbs 31:10-31:

A wife of noble character who can find?
*   She is worth far more than rubies.*
Her husband has full confidence in her
*   and lacks nothing of value.*
She brings him good, not harm,
*   all the days of her life.*
She selects wool and flax
*   and works with eager hands.*
She is like the merchant ships,
*   bringing her food from afar.*
She gets up while it is still night;
*   she provides food for her family*
*   and portions for her female servants.*
She considers a field and buys it;
*   out of her earnings she plants a vineyard.*

250

She sets about her work vigorously;
*   her arms are strong for her tasks.*
She sees that her trading is profitable,
*   and her lamp does not go out at night.*
In her hand she holds the distaff
*   and grasps the spindle with her fingers.*
She opens her arms to the poor
*   and extends her hands to the needy.*
When it snows, she has no fear for her household;
*   for all of them are clothed in scarlet.*
She makes coverings for her bed;
*   she is clothed in fine linen and purple.*
Her husband is respected at the city gate,
*   where he takes his seat among the elders of the land.*
She makes linen garments and sells them,
*   and supplies the merchants with sashes.*
She is clothed with strength and dignity;
*   she can laugh at the days to come.*
She speaks with wisdom,
*   and faithful instruction is on her tongue.*
She watches over the affairs of her household
*   and does not eat the bread of idleness.*
Her children arise and call her blessed;
*   her husband also, and he praises her:*
"Many women do noble things,
*   but you surpass them all."*
Charm is deceptive, and beauty is fleeting;
*   but a woman who fears the Lord is to be praised.*
Honor her for all that her hands have done,
*   and let her works bring her praise at the city gate.*

The passage doesn't seek to imply that women must do these specific, letter-of-the law things to be praiseworthy. It is a song of a husband, inspired by his mother, who is totally in awe of his wife's work, and the way she does things well.

If you are the husband of a minister, what your spouse's work should have a "Proverbs 31 effect" on you. It should inspire you to be a better servant of the Lord, more engaged for His purposes, and blessed to be a husband of a spouse called of the Lord. What might not be well understood by others should be well understood by you, as you see an eternal value and purpose in the spouse God has blessed you with in this life.

Reflections

- What have you heard in church about men married to ministers?

- Are all men leaders? Why or why not?

- What can we learn from looking at Deborah's husband?

- What are some ways that you, as a man, can better serve your spouse in your life?

- How can men who have spouses in ministry celebrate them for what they do?

12

TEACHING MEN TO SERVE THROUGH MEN'S MINISTRY

———————×( )×———————

FOR YOU, BRETHREN, WERE [INDEED] CALLED TO FREEDOM; ONLY [DO NOT LET YOUR] FREEDOM
BE AN INCENTIVE TO YOUR FLESH *AND* AN OPPORTUNITY *OR* EXCUSE
[FOR SELFISHNESS], BUT THROUGH LOVE YOU SHOULD SERVE ONE ANOTHER.
(GALATIANS 5:13, AMPC)

- **Reading assignment:** The Gospel of Mark

I have a confession to make. Everyone gather around.

I'm not the biggest fan of gender-specific ministries. I understand their purpose (and the Biblical context behind them), but I feel like their purpose is far removed in modern times from what they were in Bible times. In Bible times, sex-assigned ministries existed to accommodate a culture that was often divided by sex. The sexes didn't associate with one another in public. If everyone was to be served – and served well, gender-specified ministries had to exist.

Contrary to modern construct, they did not exist because anyone needed instruction in how to "be their gender." It wasn't about reinforcing gender codes or social prohibitions but finding ways to help church members navigate life as believers in society that didn't support them. As a result, the Bible's allowances were for five different areas of specialized ministry: men, women, widows, those in need, and leaders. Children's ministry is a modern construct, as are many other ministry additions we've grown accustomed to see over the years.

This isn't to say additional ministry works are bad, or that gender-specific ministry is bad. It's just not my preference, because I don't feel like it serves its original purpose anymore. That being said, regardless of how I might feel about it, the Bible does identify men's ministry. If done right, rather than create more dissention, it can be a beneficial thing, something that helps men grow and develop their faith in greater ways.

The idea of gender divided ministry is an innovative approach to ancient societal issues. It proves God can move within cultural limitations while recognizing that sometimes certain matters are better discussed among specific environments. It does matter how it's done, and it does matter why we do it. In this book, we're discussing these ministries because they give the opportunity for men to get together and learn how to serve one another in different and profound ways.

Without getting into the ins and outs of men's ministry, we are going to look at how men's ministry can be used to help men walk as better servants. Through the support, teaching, encouragement, and blessing that men can receive through this important medium, men's ministry can help create male servants rather than male spectators or dictators.

Foundations for men's ministry

Titus 2:1-2, 6-8:

But [as for] you, teach what is fitting and becoming to sound (wholesome) doctrine [the character and right living that identify true Christians].

Urge the older men to be temperate, venerable (serious), sensible, self-controlled, and sound in the faith, in the love, and in the steadfastness and patience [of Christ].

In a similar way, urge the younger men to be self-restrained and to behave prudently [taking life seriously].

And show your own self in all respects to be a pattern and a model of good deeds and works, teaching what is unadulterated, showing gravity [having the strictest regard for truth and purity of motive], with dignity and seriousness.

And let your instruction be sound and fit and wise and wholesome, vigorous and irrefutable and above censure, so that the opponent may be put to shame, finding nothing discrediting or evil to say about us. (AMPC)

I am not going to get into the specifics on how to structure and design a good men's ministry. I feel like there's enough on that out there, already. Although I probably disagree with some of it, building a men's ministry is not that deep or innovative. The foundations of the ministry within a larger one are the same as any other:

- **Leadership figure:** The men's ministry should be overseen by a man who has some level of training in men's ministry and is equipped to assist the men and develop them spiritually in the way they need.

- **Structure:** Don't assume men's ministry gatherings can just function without structure. Men's ministry activities should be planned and require volunteers to continue functioning.

- **Volunteers:** The men in a men's ministry should take turns with the required duties, and all should be available to volunteer from time to time.

- **Avoid gimmicks:** I don't think that men respond any better to gimmicks than others do. If possible, they might respond to them worse. Avoid cheesy, gimmicky slogans, names, activities, or ideas. Not all men want to go camping, hunting, or fishing. Be sincere and solid, and create a place where men truly want to go and explore faith in a deeper way with their brothers in the faith.

Purposes for men's ministry

Much of what I read about men's ministry makes me want to gag. Of course, much of what I read about any special interest ministry work makes me want to gag. We treat special interest ministry as if people are marketing gimmicks. I feel the way we approach gender-specified ministries is just more of the same, not very clever gender marketing designed to make anyone different feel like they don't belong. It seems like the extremes of men's ministry all gather around a man to make him a big, buff alpha male, stomping out his competition and demeaning others. I don't see too many other examples of men's ministry, because if there is anything we have seen in this book, it seems like people are very uncomfortable with the idea of a man who doesn't fall into the clear category of a tough guy ready to tackle the world as a leader.

Just as women's ministry shouldn't stereotype women, men's ministry shouldn't stereotype men, either. There should be a genuine call and concern for men to develop more of the characteristics of Christ in their lives, even if it means elevating Christian character above worldly concepts and traditions of what manhood is about.

- Encourage one another.
- Pray for one another.
- Facilitate friendships and fellowships among the men of the church.
- Tackle issues that men encounter from a Scriptural perspective.
- Edify men as they face general issues that are part of the Christian life.
- Teach how to be a good example.
- Train for different stages of men's lives: singlehood, fatherhood, marriage, widower, divorced.

- Training for service, including service projects.
- Teach men about interaction with the Christian life, in ways that they can ask questions and feel comfortable enough to discuss and explore.

Romans 15:5:

May God, Who gives you this endurance and encouragement, allow you to live in harmony with each other by following the example of Christ Jesus. (GW)

1 Thessalonians 5:10-11:

He died for us so that, whether we are awake in this life or asleep in death, we will live together with Him. Therefore, encourage each other and strengthen one another as you are doing. (GW)

Men can tell when a ministry specifically targeting them will turn into a ridiculous, cheesy attempt to bolster manhood. I believe this is one of the key reasons why men tend to avoid things such as men's ministry (and it also defies the reason men don't want to come to church is because of women, since women aren't at a men's ministry event). For a men's ministry to work, men must get something out of it that they can't get from something else in their lives. Any man can spend Thursday night playing poker with his buddies or watching an adventure-thriller type movie. They can't get true fellowship, instruction in living, or development in the Christian life from such activities. This means that men's ministry facilitators need to dial down the extensive cheerleading that often goes into them, trying too hard to prove that being a man is all right. Men already are good with being men, but what they need to become good with is being Christian men who know how to be servants.

Keeping men encouraged

As much as I love being a Christian, I can't deny that

sometimes it can feel like a bit of a drag. Day passes into day and the excitement and change we hoped to be part of our conversions doesn't materialize in the way we expected. Friends and family come and go, many misunderstand where we are in the Lord, and may attack us in our faith. Sometimes it even comes from other believers, especially the ones we thought would never leave nor forsake us. When you try so hard to do the right thing, service sometimes gets pushed to the background. You're busy managing life, right at that moment.

Then you have the reality that service isn't always accepted by others in the way we hope it will. There are plenty of times I tried to assist or serve someone only to have them livid, throwing something back in my face because it wasn't done the way they wanted. If you are a man trying to live this Christian life in the proper way and do the right things, there are going to be a lot of times where you find yourself disillusioned and seeking answers.

Galatians 6:9-10:

Let us not become weary in doing good, for at the proper time we will reap a harvest if we do not give up. Therefore, as we have opportunity, let us do good to all people, especially to those who belong to the family of believers.

Colossians 3:23-24:

Whatever you do, work at it with all your heart, as working for the Lord, not for human masters, since you know that you will receive an inheritance from the Lord as a reward. It is the Lord Christ you are serving.

This is right where men's ministry should come into full view. Even if a men's minister or group doesn't have all the answers, they should be there to offer support and encouragement during times like these. Men need encouragement to push beyond immediate things and into the deeper aspects of the Christian life, such as service. They need to be re-focused on things that are important and not give up in discouragement as they go along.

Men serving other men

Ministry specifically for men should address the issue of servanthood for men in a way that breaks down barriers and stereotypes often heard about men's service. Men's ministry is the perfect place to clarify that men serving other men is a necessary part of the Christian life and doesn't mean or imply anything about the men who serve. Service among men, for other men, does not make a man demeaned, less of a man, weak, or any other things people say it does. It makes him more of a man, a better man, and better able to reach out and care about other people because he has purposed himself to heavenly things.

As believers, we need to get over the concept that serving is going to hurt or demoralize us. Service is one of the biggest spiritual edifiers we have. It teaches and trains us for eternity. The attitude that service is beneath men because it destroys their masculinity is destroying their faith. If you are not man enough to serve, you are not man enough.

Mark 9:35:

And He sat down and called the Twelve [apostles], and He said to them, If anyone desires to be first, he must be last of all, and servant of all. (AMPC)

Philippians 2:1-4:

Therefore if you have any encouragement from being united with Christ, if any comfort from His love, if any common sharing in the Spirit, if any tenderness and compassion, then make my joy complete by being like-minded, having the same love, being one in spirit and of one mind. Do nothing out of selfish ambition or vain conceit. Rather, in humility value others above yourselves, not looking to your own interests but each of you to the interests of the others.

The competition that exists between men in society is a large part of the reason why men don't like the idea of serving one another. To serve another man is seen as a sign of subordination, one where competition is over and the one who serves walks away in defeat. This couldn't be further from the truth. It means putting on the new mind of Christ, being willing to become the new man rather than just talk about the new man. Men's ministry is the perfect place for this transformation, because it can be done in a comfortable atmosphere, one that understands and empathizes with the unique challenges men face as pertains to servanthood and walking out the disciplines of the Christian life.

By learning to serve other men, men can break through barriers and stigmas that keep them from reaching out (more times than not) out of pride and arrogance. Servanthood not only shows vulnerability, but it also acknowledges it in others. None of us is an island, and servanthood proves once and for all that God has created us for connection, one to another. Just as all genders need supportive friends, men need that same support amongst themselves. As people, service bridges that barrier, the gulf that says, "I can do it myself!" when we really do need that hand of help to get us through.

That's why service is so important to us as believers: not only is it humbling to the person who gives service, it is also humbling to the one who receives it. Service as a Kingdom principle reminds us that God gives to us by His grace, not what we deserve, but what we truly need. Service, therefore, is a constant reminder of what God has done for us and what He does in others, and He gives us the unique opportunity to walk that out in our everyday lives.

Group service

Men's ministry is a great place for men to work in church or community service projects together, facilitating the need for men to serve others beyond themselves. We should never, ever forget that men do have the responsibility to serve God, their churches, one another, their spouses, and their families, but service doesn't start and end there. Sometimes I think we talk so much about serving those who are most immediate and convenient, we forget that service isn't just about those who are around us or closest to us. God commands us to be available to serve our neighbor, serve other people, and serve unto Him, whether it is among those we know the best, or among those that we might never see again.

Luke 10:25-37:

On one occasion an expert in the law stood up to test Jesus.

"Teacher," he asked, "what must I do to inherit eternal life?"

"What is written in the Law?" He replied. "How do you read it?"

He answered, "'Love the Lord your God with all your heart and with all your soul and with all your strength and with all your mind'; and, 'Love your neighbor as yourself.'"

"You have answered correctly," Jesus replied. "Do this and you will live."

But he wanted to justify himself, so he asked Jesus, "And who is my neighbor?"

In reply Jesus said: "A man was going down from Jerusalem to Jericho, when he was attacked by robbers. They stripped him of his clothes, beat him and went away, leaving him half dead. A priest happened to be going down the same road, and when he saw the man, he passed by on the other side. So too, a Levite, when he came to the place and saw him, passed by on the other side. But a Samaritan, as he traveled, came where the man was; and when he saw him, he took pity on him. He went to him and bandaged his wounds, pouring on oil and wine. Then he put the man on his own donkey, brought him to an inn and took care of him. The next day he took out two denarii and gave them to the innkeeper. 'Look after him,' he said, 'and when I return, I will reimburse you for any extra expense you may have.'

"Which of these three do you think was a neighbor to the man who fell into the hands of robbers?"

The expert in the law replied, "The one who had mercy on him."

Jesus told him, "Go and do likewise."

Men's ministries should not spend all their time sitting around, watching movies and staring at each other awkwardly as the facilitator tries to teach them how to hug and share feelings. Men are traditionally spoken of as being doers, thus men should do something when they are in men's ministry settings. Community service projects, building projects, church maintenance, hospital visits, service to the leaders of the church, etc. are all areas where service should start and launch, encouraging the men in the church to be active and engaged in what is going on in the world around them.

Training our sons to serve

Men's ministry is one of the first training grounds for young men to learn how important service is within their lives and faith. From the time children are young, they are already treated differently across gender lines. We assume a preacher's sons will be the ones to follow in his footsteps, rather than considering his daughters might be equally interested. We encourage girls to be domestic and to do chores for their brothers, and we punish boys less for committed infractions. Boys are encouraged to be like their dads, which means if a dad or male figure is not engaged in church work, doesn't serve, sits back and surveys, and has the attitude that being present is enough for them, it's not so farfetched to wonder why boys grow up to be men who are disinterested in service and community involvement.

We also are quick to complain about the state of boys today: they are disrespectful to authority, don't dress properly, treat women poorly, are dismissive of other genders or non-heteronormative sexual orientations, have problems focusing and concentrating, and are disinterested in proper conduct. What we don't consider is these boys learned this from somewhere: whether it is due to being overindulged and spoiled, getting the message that the world owes them something, or just a general defiant attitude, these boys got the message that it is better to receive than give, to be treated special than to be fair and just, and that we should all give them what they seek because they are who they are.

Malachi 4:6:

He will turn the hearts of the parents to their children, and the hearts of the children to their parents; or else I will come and strike the land with total destruction.

Matthew 10:42:

And if anyone gives even a cup of cold water to one of these little ones who is My disciple, truly I tell you, that person will certainly not lose their reward.

Ephesians 6:1-4:

Children, obey your parents in the Lord, for this is right. "Honor your father and mother"—which is the first commandment with a promise— "so that it may go well with you and that you may enjoy long life on the earth."

Fathers, do not exasperate your children; instead, bring them up in the training and instruction of the Lord.

1 Thessalonians 2:11-12:

For you know that we dealt with each of you as a father

deals with his own children, encouraging, comforting and urging you to live lives worthy of God, Who calls you into His kingdom and glory.

We love prophecies about sons turning toward fathers and fathers turning toward sons as well as words about good relationships between parents and children, but I think we forget that service is involved in such statements. Many aren't willing to take the steps to do it. It takes effort, a father to go first, to see the hearts of the fathers and sons turn toward one another. We like to talk about things, but we ignore that God often works through us. If we aren't willing to do what God has called us to do, we won't see the results we hope for.

A good men's ministry can turn a lot of the problems we have with boys and young men around...if the men in the group are willing to do the job of participating and living it out in their lives. If a boy can see his dad or other men (it doesn't have to be a biological parent, although it's great if there is one in the picture), involved not just by himself, but with other men, in doing things for other people, many of these barriers can be overcome and stigmas removed. Men's ministry can involve boys and young men of the church as is appropriate and can get them on the path to seeing servanthood as an integral part of the life of a man. This can, then, follow them throughout life instead of them picking it up and putting it on. When brutish behaviors are displayed in a boy, the men's ministry can be there to help check such behaviors. If a father figure is absent, the men of the church can help to be there for that boy or young man. If a boy is more sensitive, spiritual, or quiet, they can be aided and developed into their calling and future as a man of God, a servant of the Lord and of mankind.

<u>Service can change the world</u>

We talk a good game in Christianity today. We complain about where things are and where they are heading, but we don't do anything to turn that tide. There's so much about men and developing men today, but we aren't asking enough of men. We don't require them to grow and change to become like Christ. We complain about the world's values, then encourage them in our boys and men. We talk about wanting change, but we don't offer solutions, and then we never change.

Isaiah 58:9-11:

Then you will call, and the Lord will answer;
you will cry for help, and He will say: Here am I.

f you do away with the yoke of oppression,
with the pointing finger and malicious talk,
and if you spend yourselves in behalf of the hungry
and satisfy the needs of the oppressed,
then your light will rise in the darkness,
and your night will become like the noonday.
The Lord will guide you always;
He will satisfy your needs in a sun-scorched land
and will strengthen your frame.
You will be like a well-watered garden,
like a spring whose waters never fail.

God is calling you, man of God, man of faith, man of valor, to rise and take your place as His servant. If you want to change the world, the person you need to start with is yourself. You can blame your spouse, your stupid boss, your kids, or your pastor, or you can realize that maybe God has called you to start making that difference by serving other people in a deeper way. If you falter, there's no shame in picking up and starting again. You might not figure it all out right away, but when all is said and done, it'll be worth it. God's words to us on judgment day won't be "Well done, good and faithful...."

- Man
- Leader
- Minister
- Parent

- Ephesians 4:11 minister
- Elder
- Teacher
- Professional
- Gifted songwriter
- Musician
- Policeman
- Businessman
- Judge
- Lawyer
- Rich man
- Alpha male

...and so on and so forth, but...

"His master replied, 'Well done, good and faithful servant! You have been faithful with a few things; I will put you in charge of many things. Come and share your master's happiness!' (Matthew 25:23)

At the end of the day, that is what you are called to be: servant. However you are called to serve, that is exactly who God has appointed you to be. The sooner you embrace it, the sooner you will be able to embark on this wonderful journey to eternity that He has in store, just for you, as a man of God.

Reflections

- How do you feel about men's ministry? Does your church have a program?

- What would you say is the most important purpose of any men's ministry?

- How can a men's ministry help men keep encouraged?

- What are some projects that a men's ministry can

take on for the church or community?

- How can men's ministry turn around the tide for many of the issues we see with boys and young men?

ABOUT THE AUTHOR

―――――――――――――――( )―――――――――――――――

DR. LEE ANN B. MARINO, PH.D., D.MIN., D.D.

Dr. Lee Ann B. Marino, Ph.D., D.Min., D.D. (she/her) is "everyone's favorite theologian" leading Gen X, Millennials, and Gen Z with expertise in leadership training, queer and feminist theology, general religion, and apostolic theology. She has served in ministry since 1998 and was ordained as a pastor in 2002 and an apostle in 2010. She founded what is now Sanctuary Apostolic Fellowship Empowerment (SAFE) Ministries in 2004. Under her ministry heading Dr. Marino is founder and Overseer of Sanctuary International Fellowship Tabernacle (SIFT) (the original home of National Coming Out Sunday) and The Sanctuary Network, and Chancellor of Apostolic Covenant Theological Seminary (ACTS).

Affectionately nicknamed "the Spitfire," Dr. Marino has spent over two decades as an "apostle, preacher, and teacher" (2 Timothy 1:11), exercising her personal mandate to become "all things to all people" (1 Corinthians 9:22). Her embrace of spiritual issues (both technical and intimate) has found its home among both seekers and believers, those who desire spiritual answers to today's issues.

Dr. Marino has preached throughout the United States, Puerto Rico, and Europe in hundreds of religious services and experiences throughout the years. A history maker in her own right, she has spent over two decades in advocacy, education, and work for and within minority spiritual communities (including African American, Hispanic, and LGBTQ+). She has also served as the first woman on all-male synods, councils, and panels, as well as the first preacher or speaker welcomed of a different race, sexual orientation, or identity among diverse communities. Today, Dr. Marino's work extends to over 150 countries as she hosts the popular *Kingdom Now* podcast, which is in the top 20 percentile of all podcasts worldwide. She is also the author of over 35 books and the popular Patheos column, *Leadership on Fire*. To date, she has had five bestselling titles within their subject matter: *Understanding Demonology, Spiritual Warfare, Healing, and Deliverance: A Manual for the Christian Minister; Ministry School Boot Camp: Training for Helps Ministries, Appointments, and Beyond; Discovering Intimacy: A Journey Through the Song of Solomon; Fruit of the Vine: Study and Commentary on the Fruit of the Spirit;* and *Ministering to LGBTQ+ (and Those Who Love Them): A Primer for Queer Theology* (and its accompanying workbook).

As a public icon and social media influencer, Dr. Marino advocates healthy body image (curvy/full-figured), representation as a demisexual/aromantic, and albinism awareness as a model. Known to those she works with, she is a spiritual mom, teacher, leader, professor, confidant, and friend. She continues to transform, receiving new teaching, revelation, and insight in this thing we call "ministry." Through years of spiritual growth and maturity, Dr. Marino stands as herself, here to present what God has given to her for any who have an ear to hear.

For more information, visit her website at kingdompowernow.org.